HIPPOS,
A MONGOOSE
& ME

To my friend

Meghan

Hope you enjoy the
read and the trip!

Rudi

HIPPOS,
A MONGOOSE
& ME

*Tales of rescue and survival
in the wilds of Africa*

Karen Paolillo

PENGUIN BOOKS

Published by Penguin Books,
an imprint of Penguin Random House South Africa (Pty) Ltd
Reg. No. 1953/000441/07
The Estuaries No. 4, Oxbow Crescent, Century Avenue, Century City, 7441
PO Box 1144, Cape Town, 8000 South Africa
www.penguinrandomhouse.co.za

Penguin
Random House
South Africa

First published 2024

1 3 5 7 9 10 8 6 4 2

Publication © Penguin Random House 2024
Text © Karen Paolillo 2024

PUBLISHER: Pippa Parker
MANAGING EDITOR: Roelien Theron
EDITOR: Helen de Villiers
COVER DESIGNER: Sheryl Buckley
TYPESETTER: Deirdré Geldenhuys

Photographs © Karen Paolillo

Set in 11 pt on 14 pt Sabon LT Std

Printed by **novus print**, a division of Novus Holdings

MIX
Paper | Supporting
responsible forestry
FSC® C022948

ISBN 978 1 77989 001 6 (print)
ISBN 978 1 77989 002 3 (ePub)

To all the Turgwe hippos, and young Steve in particular, for accepting me into their wild life. And to our beloved Squiggle, the slender mongoose who captured our hearts and souls – I will see you again, my beauty.

Contents

Contents

Acknowledgements

Thanks to Pippa Parker, publisher of Struik Nature, for accepting my manuscript for publication. Your faith in *Hippos, a Mongoose and me* means the world to me and the animals.

To the wonderful editor Helen de Villiers who helped me so much to show off the animals in the best of ways. I have loved your work ethic and the text came together so beautifully.

To Hilary Johnson in the UK, you were with me for *A Hippo Love Story* and you believed in this next project, shaping my sentences and sorting out the lack of commas and dots. Thank you Hilary for what you do for the greyhounds and all the other dogs, you are one special lady.

To Laura Simpson of the Harmony Fund USA, supporting the Turgwe Hippo Trust (THT) every month with your wonderful aid for the Rangers. We love you for your caring, your help and your ongoing belief in what we do.

To the now-retired directors of Friends of Turgwe Hippos in Canada, especially to Andrew Clarke for all that you did for the hippos; and a special mention to Steve Gordon who still sends all my adoption videos for me.

Massive thanks to The Friends of the Hippos directors in the USA: Cinda, Nina, Charles, Teresa and Kay – without you the Trust would not exist; and special huge hippo hugs and love to Cinda Lautenschlegar who organised the charity in the US and got us a 501c3 number. Cinda, you are one in a million.

To Mark Powell in the UK, thank you so much for always sending my videos to YouTube and for placing them on the website under Turgwe Hippo Mark. Also for being our personal taxi service in the UK!

To Mirinda Thorpe of Australia who came to the THT as a volunteer and is now the THT's official house sitter – somebody I can completely trust to run everything back at home and look after all the animals, allowing us also to have a break. Miri, we both love you dearly.

To everyone who has adopted a Turgwe Hippo, donated or purchased merchandise, and helped when I have sent out appeals, without your financial support our work could not continue. We salute you all.

I thank sincerely the Rangers, presently Peter, Elijah, Tapera, Alphonse, Derek and Thomas; and, of course, my right-hand man Silas Matyarutsa. You are all part of the team that keeps not just the hippos but all of the wildlife in this area alive.

To my best friend, the amazing animal sculptor Suzie Marsh of Cornwall, UK – thank you for always being there for me and opening up your home to us when we need some clean sea air to refresh our spirits. We love you too.

To Sarah Carter, Twala Trust Zimbabwe – thank you for always contacting me when my pain is at its rawest, and knowing how it feels. I value your friendship highly and love you for who you are.

To all on social media, Facebook and Instagram who follow the Turgwe Hippo Trust and have the kindness to comment and bolster my flagging spirits when, at times, things become extremely hard to bear, thank you for caring.

I thank with all my heart the three professional actors who have signed on to be Patrons of the Turgwe Hippo Trust – Dan Richardson, Peter Egan and Mark Bonnar. Thank you all for having faith in me and caring about the Turgwe Hippos.

Last but not least to Jean-Roger Paolillo. Your passions are not the same as mine, yet here you are three decades down the line and we are still together, holding hands. I thank you for allowing me to be who I am, and love you for being who you are. We have found that by standing apart we can often join together and do something worthwhile that is much bigger than ourselves. Your strength, luck and single-mindedness have kept this Trust going.

With my love – Karen and all the hippos and other animals

Zimbabwe, Hippo Haven, Turgwe Hippo Trust, October 2023

To contribute to the Turgwe Hippo Trust please go to
www.savethehippos.info or visit Facebook **Karen Paolillo**
or **Turgwe Hippo Trust,** or Instagram **the_turgwe_hippo_trust**

Prologue

In my world the days move too fast. One minute you think it's 2018, the next time you look it's five years down the road. I have been asked by some of the Turgwe Hippo Trust (THT) supporters who follow our activities on social media if I would write a sequel to my book, *A Hippo Love Story*, published by Penguin in 2014.

I have been contemplating for a while how to put this second book together. In my first book I ran through the first two decades in the bush, telling the story of how Jean-Roger, my husband, and I live a relatively primitive life in the south-eastern part of Zimbabwe compared with what we call the real world. It was a story that wrenched at my heart in the telling as there were events that were not just adventures but that often held terror and fear. Those experiences of living such a very different existence were at times extremely hard to write about. Even on reading what I did finally write made me realise that I could not accept so much of what had occurred in those years; but that somehow we had come through it all and are still actively working for the safety of the hippos and all the other animals in our life here in Zimbabwe.

Living in the bush and doing your utmost to protect wildlife in Africa is not for the faint-hearted. It demands a strong character and the ability to persevere and stay determined. Ordinary days full of African sun and the scents and sights of beauty can suddenly be interrupted by life-threatening events. There are more insidious dangers too: it is so easy to catch one of Africa's maladies and end up thinking that this time the malaria really is going to kill you. Or that tick-bite fever is just too much to bear.

Worst of all is when politics rears its ugly head, and then everything changes. Suddenly, hospitable, mostly smiling, happy people, are told by their politicians to behave like monsters. Sometimes they are ordered to hurt you or even try to kill you. That part in *A Hippo Love Story* was the hardest section to write. Despite this, though, I managed to end that book in a positive way, with hope.

That hope has been rewarded time and time again. Here we are, nearly 10 years down the track, and still we live our lives with and for these hippos, as well as so many other wild animals. The stories of day-to-day life with these animals could stretch to an odyssey, but we mortals have little time in this world now for the written word. Raised on social media, our attention spans are short. We use so many platforms as we scroll, discard, like, love and leave, all in a matter of minutes. So I thought, okay, I need to continue telling the story of these hippos but in a different way – why not talk about some of the special stories? Read a paragraph and then take a break, coming back to another story when time permits. I won't write about just the hippos but also about many of the other wild animals that have made their mark in this amazing life we lead. The stories range from glorious to devastating, some offering moments of sheer light, others of great sadness and pain. My aim is to tell how it happened, but always leave the reader with hope, which is my philosophy.

None of us ever passes through life in a bubble of constancy and happiness. We all at times stumble and some, sadly, find it very hard to pull themselves back up off the floor to keep going. So perhaps these stories will help to bring light, laughter and yes, sometimes tears. Tears are not always bad: they can heal wounds, help alleviate grief, or even take away some of our own problems if the tears are for somebody else.

I try to focus on the good, to find kindness in life and, if possible, in other people. That is possibly one of life's hardest challenges. Thankfully, as a lover of animals, I find it's the animals that help me again and again. Not just the amazing hippos, but every other special animal that has moved in and out of my life.

Here in the bushveld we have no permanent electricity, our drinking water has to be collected from 19 kilometres away. It's a natural landscape without signs of man-made intervention. No telephone or power lines, nothing to show human 'progress', just Nature. Some people, having read *A Hippo Love Story*, tell me that my husband, Jean-Roger, is a unique man to stay living as we do in the bush, sharing a life centred on my passion. We do, though, share some traits, one being our need for space – this wild space that encompasses our home, Hippo Haven, and the areas that we work in. Also, there is this love that we have together that's so in sync in many ways, as we do not like the pressures of the world. I suppose most important is our need to be our own people, each separate from the other and yet joined.

Jean's passion is for anything airplane-related, whether he is flying one, building tiny miniature model aircraft, or using his encyclopaedic knowledge of every plane ever built, learning from his array of books and his deep love for that particular machine; whereas my life is dedicated to continue helping the hippos and other wildlife indefinitely.

We agree to differ in our passions. Jean's humour and luck, teamed with my dogged determination and complete devotion to what I do, have taken us together along this bush trail. We are on a long walk through the wild, accompanied by a vast assortment of animals and experiences that have taught us how to live our lives to the absolute full.

I

Maladies and miracles

Back in the early nineties, before the inception of the Turgwe Hippo Trust (THT), we lived under the umbrella of my French husband's profession, geology. Jean-Roger was employed by the huge mining concern Rio Tinto to explore the area for gold and diamonds. British born, I had followed a childhood dream of coming to Africa to work with wildlife, and had trained as a professional safari guide, becoming the first girl in Zimbabwe to pass the Safari Guides' National Park Professional Licence. This allowed me to take tourists on foot or horseback into the bush to photograph and learn about the animals of this extraordinary land.

It was 1991 and Jean and I were camped above the Turgwe River, living in a lean-to that we had made: an open-fronted canvas dwelling with corrugated iron sheets for the roof. The mining company had provided us with a small caravan, but we didn't like the idea of living inside it, especially as we had arrived in October, the hottest time of the year in the Lowveld. We used the caravan as a kitchen. Jean's staff, who were local African people, lived at the other end of the camp in wood prefab huts that the mining company provided.

Our lean-to home was attached to the caravan where our four cats and small cocker spaniel, Sammy, would live at night. We had made a wire run leading from a caravan window so the cats could go out at night and do their business inside a protective wire cage, safe from predators like leopards, lions or hyenas. We slept, ate and lived under our canvas awning with its open-fronted view across

1

the expanse of the Turgwe River. As we lay in bed at the start of the day the dawn light would reveal a vista of the Turgwe River and surrounding bush. Awakening us every morning was the flypast of a flock of up to 22 Hadeda ibis storks, shouting out their early morning *ha ha, de de, da da* call.

On our southern boundary there's nothing but pristine bush, mainly made up of mopane forests, with massive leadwood and knob thorn trees. Behind the forest some huge rock koppies (hills) act as back-lighting to an artist's canvas on days when rain is about to fall. The cumulus clouds turn a deep dark grey with a slight blue sheen. As they encircle the koppies, a dream-like light illuminates the granite rock, kissing it with a golden glow that lasts for only a matter of seconds and is impossible to capture on camera.

Not far from our tented home lived the Turgwe hippos, our nearest large mammal neighbours. In the mornings they would announce their presence as they returned to their river pools after being out most of the night grazing and filling their gigantic stomachs with grass. In the late afternoon they would wake up from a day of digesting the grasses, and set off to graze again through the night.

On this particular morning I was still in bed as I had malaria. Jean-Roger had been hit by it as well, five days previously, but this morning he had made it out of bed at his usual time as he was feeling a lot more like himself.

The first time I caught malaria I lost just over seven kilograms in weight over a period of one week. My fever was so high that eventually my employer drove me to the nearest local clinic, fearing that I was going to die. I survived, but unfortunately malaria can recur, either the same strain or a completely new one. The Lowveld is a malaria area and the disease regularly claims many African people's lives, generally those who have no access to medicine.

Jean was busily making a cup of tea on the campfire when Dai Dai, an African man living close to our camp, called out to him. Dai Dai worked as pump man for our nearest neighbours, the Whittalls, whose homestead was about 19 kilometres away on the property known as Humani. He would pump water from the river using their diesel-run pump to fill up brick tanks situated on the top of a 60-metre-high koppie. These tanks enabled Roger Whittall to gravity-feed water to his cattle troughs, which were dotted about in the bush. The pipes carrying river water up to the tanks were buried in deep underground channels to stop elephants from digging them up.

Jean came back to my bed and, seeing I was awake, said, 'Dai Dai has just told me that there is a leopard in one of the tanks on top of the koppie and that when he went up there to check if the pump was working he heard the animal growling. He said he ran like hell all the way down the hill to come and tell us. He has no idea what to do. The pump was still operating as he was talking to me, so I immediately told him to run down to the river and turn it off. If that leopard is in the tank it may already have drowned. Those tanks are over three metres deep.'

I was relatively clear headed as it was by now my third day of malaria, and I could eat a bit without feeling nauseous. But there was no way I would be capable of walking, and definitely not of climbing up a koppie. 'Jean, are you feeling strong enough to go up there and find out what's going on? If you hand me my camera so I can load it with film, you can photograph what you see. But please go and save that leopard. And if you can, also get some photos.'

'How do you expect me to save it, Karen? It's a bloody leopard!' Jean grumbled.

'Use your excellent brain to figure it out, my love. I am really not well enough to even think it out, let alone help you, but you have to save it, please.'

Unimpressed, Jean grimaced, but grunted that he would give it a try, and went off to put on his climbing shoes. Then, taking the camera from me, he gave a thumbs-up and left, and I slipped back into sleep. Malaria really does knock you out. Just a simple conversation can hurt your head and make it feel it's about to explode.

The next thing I knew, I was being woken by Jean nudging me, looking pleased with himself. I was instantly intrigued. 'What happened? Did you help the leopard? Is it okay? Did you get photos? Tell me!' I was fighting dizziness, but I just had to know.

'Well, Dai Dai came up the koppie with me as I wasn't sure if I would make the climb on my own. Even though the malaria has shifted, my head was spinning quite a bit. After just the walk to the foot of the koppie my shoes seemed to behave as though they were filled with sand and my legs felt very heavy. I made it to the top in the slowest time ever. At the top I could hear a very loud growling, but it didn't seem to be coming from the tank; instead, it seemed to come from that large Cape fig tree. Dai Dai refused to go near the tank, so it was up to me. I managed to climb up the side using the built-in footholds in the concrete, and you cannot imagine what happened next!

'Down at the bottom of the tank in about half a metre of water were two tiny leopard cubs. One had brown eyes and the other's were blue. Karen, they were just the cutest things you could imagine. Before I even had a plan I couldn't resist using up the whole reel of film, they were just so picture perfect, with the sunlight shining on them.

'Thank God I had got Dai Dai to stop pumping. The cubs were not happy, and just stared up at me. Then I realised in my over-enthusiasm of getting photos that the growling was not stopping and, if anything, it seemed to be getting louder.

'I remembered what you told me about how leopards can be extremely aggressive when they have cubs, and there I was, standing three metres above two cubs that were trapped, and whose mum was mighty pissed-off. So what was I to do?

'All I could think of was to cut a branch that was thick and long enough to put in the tank as a ramp, and hope that the cubs would then be able to climb up and out. I got down from the tank and all the while I was talking soothingly to what I assumed must be the mother, somewhere up in the fig tree.

'Fortunately, I had remembered to bring the machete, and I headed back to Dai Dai, who was looking decidedly unhappy about having to hang around. I explained my plan and he agreed, and together we cut down a thickish branch. But Dai Dai made it clear he was not going to help drag the branch to the tank – I would have to drag it and hoist it inside the tank on my own. So, with the malaria threatening to sap me of all strength, and the shakiness in my limbs getting worse, and my head spinning, I dragged the cut branch to the tank and managed to haul it up and push it down inside.'

I was mesmerised, with even my own state of health forgotten as I listened to Jean. 'Then what happened?' I demanded, desperate to know if the cubs got out.

'Well, I backed away and waited for a few minutes. Absolutely nothing happened – and then the mother let out a huge, gruff kind of grunt-growl, as though instructing her cubs to make a move. To my astonishment, a cub appeared at the rim of the tank and within seconds it had leapt down and was running full speed towards the fig tree. I was so pleased! I waited for cub number two to follow. Nothing happened. No movement, nothing. So all I could do was go back and see what had happened. I pulled myself back up, using the footholds, and there were two blue eyes peering up, but not moving. So down I went again, got Dai Dai to cut a much thinner branch, and I headed back up to the top of the tank with it. I began to poke the branch at the cub, and do you know what happened?'

'Tell me! I can't stand the suspense!'

'Well, the cub started *playing* with the branch, batting at it as if this was just one big fun game. By this time, the mother had started up her grunt-growling again. I was getting nervous, thinking she might decide to come over to find out what the delay was. So I must admit I gave the cub a bit of a shove up his backside with the branch. This had the desired effect: it not only hurried towards the other branch, but climbed up it and leapt down not more than a foot from me, and then ran straight off to the fig tree. Wow, was I a happy man! I can't wait for you to see my photos. I'll put the film in the fridge to keep it cool until we can get it developed the next time we go to town.'

Jean was beaming and very pleased with himself and I was proud of him for saving the cubs' lives. They would never have managed to get out on their own. If the mother had tried to jump in to help them she would have been trapped as well. I opened the camera while Jean went to the fire to put the kettle on – and I blanched.

I couldn't believe what I found. My brain told me I had loaded the film, but malaria had fogged my actions, and the camera was absolutely empty. I found the film tucked up in the bedclothes. I must have suffered a lapse when trying to load the camera and this was the result. Oh my God, I thought, how do I tell Jean?

He reappeared and suddenly found his wife being extra kind and full of praise for his rescue operation, which is not at all my style. He smelt a rat!

'Karen, what is going on? You are acting very strange and nothing like your normal self.' Jean knows me so well!

'My love, I stuffed up. In my incapacitated state I didn't load the film. I am so, so sorry.'

He looked at me, looked down, and then up again and burst into laughter. 'Well, I have the memories, but now nobody will ever credit me if I can't produce the evidence. I will have to get Dai Dai to back me up.' He hugged me, told me to sleep, and that was the end of the drama for that particular morning.

2

How it began

Fate clearly played a role in my meeting with Jean-Roger. Sometimes a person enters your life and, however fleeting the moment, something resonates deep inside you, telling you that this is someone special. The feeling is too good to let go and you will do almost anything to keep the connection alive. In our case this might have proved difficult as we were separated by the Mediterranean Sea. We had met in Malinda in Kenya, on a glass-bottomed boat taking tourists out to view the fish and snorkel in the Indian Ocean. I was living in Zimbabwe and Jean-Roger worked for the multinational Shell as an oil geologist. At that time he was living and working in the north of the Netherlands.

However, we had both felt this strong connection, and our relationship was destined to succeed. Jean, on his return to Holland, had written asking me to come and visit him for a holiday. Three months later I found myself on a plane, taking a trip that would change my world completely but, strangely enough, would eventually lead me back into the life that I had always dreamed of living – here in the bush.

It was not easy establishing our home. Initially we were here as unwanted visitors. Mining companies in Zimbabwe, having secured an environmental impact assessment, can set up on any private land without the permission of the property owner. In our case, in 1990, this area was made up of individual cattle ranches, varying from 18,000 to over 200,000 acres. They were owned either by established families like the Whittalls, whose parents had been the first pioneers in the area, or by individual companies. The land had always remained wild, with only these people ranching their cattle, so it didn't require much management. Most of the ranchers allowed their cattle to roam freely across large areas of bush, which were fenced into massive paddocks. They employed local people to stay with the cattle and camp alongside the herds, each week rounding up the animals to bring them into a central area for dipping, deworming and other such treatments.

Alongside the cattle were the natural inhabitants of the area – the wildlife. Cattle and predators do not happily coexist, so over the years, long before we had arrived, many lions, leopards and hyenas had been killed by the local ranchers. Elephants were also killed at that time, the ranch owners complaining that they regularly knocked down the fences. The buffalo, too, had been targeted, as they carried diseases that cattle could contract.

What the ranchers had gradually discovered, however, was that the habitat was not suited to cattle ranching, no matter how much they messed with the natural wildlife. Cattle are susceptible to diseases that do not affect the wildlife. But, even more importantly, the Lowveld has always been drought-prone and is one of the driest and hottest areas in Zimbabwe. And when a drought hit, the stock would die in their hundreds. Cattle ranching was not a long-term plan that would prosper.

So, just before we arrived, all the various owners of land in the area – presiding over some 23 properties – had got together and formed a coalition. They decided that they would all drop their individual boundary fences, phase out their herds of cattle and go back to making a business based on the original inhabitants of the land, the wildlife. This heralded the establishment in 1991 of the Save Valley Conservancy.

Then the 1992 drought hit and everything was put on hold as people struggled to keep their livelihoods afloat. This meant they had to feed whatever cattle they still owned, and in some cases even some of the wildlife. The Whittalls fed their rhinos as this species is endangered. They were fortunate in having underground water and huge boreholes, so they had the capacity to feed the cattle and wildlife with some of the crops that they grew.

I had already approached the Whittalls about permission to try to feed the hippos below our camp, and they had agreed. So I began the feeding programme and managed to keep alive the 13 hippos remaining in the Turgwe River. I had found out about what to feed the hippos by speaking on the phone to people running zoos overseas, and also to some experts within Zimbabwe. Nobody had ever fed wild hippos in the bush long-term, but most had ideas on what to feed them on a short-term basis.

It turned out that much of the information I was given was incorrect; for instance, the amount of food suggested for an adult hippo was only about a third of what was actually necessary. I ended up feeding them over a ton of food each night, the bulk of it a hay, called Rhodes grass or soya bean hay. All of this I had to have transported by 30-ton trucks that I hired from the other side of Harare, the capital, which often entailed a two-day drive just to get to us. Harare is over 450 kilometres away.

The hay was mixed with survival ration, which was made up of maize offcuts, cotton seed and molasses and was meant for feeding cattle. Because it didn't have any urea in it, it was perfectly safe for hippos. I hoped it would attract the hippos with the scent of its sugary content. I added horse cubes or game nuts as an extra protein and the 13 hippos I fed ended up in such good condition that two females conceived during this time.

One of the calves was Tembia, son of Bob, and he was born just after the drought in June 1993. He eventually became the dominant bull at a pool in the Turgwe upstream from our home, moving there in 2004 at the age of 11 and starting his own family (see chapter 20, Tembia hippo).

To save the lives of the hippos and many other wild animals in the 1992 drought, apart from feeding them, we had to address the growing problem with their river water. The Turgwe River was shrinking, and eventually dried up completely. So we built the first cemented pan, designed by Jean-Roger. We dug out a large area of over seven metres in length, resulting in a huge hippo swimming pool. It had cemented walls and a rock-covered floor, also cemented. We pumped water into it by laying a very long pipeline of over 19 kilometres to Roger Whittall's boreholes. The pan was just under two metres deep at one end and half a metre at the other, so the hippos could wade in and then completely submerge. We also built them a trough nearby for drinking water.

I had another drinking trough built for the then 'bachelor' bull, Happy, as Bob wouldn't allow him near the pan or trough used by the other hippos. It was Happy's trough that enabled me to record what an adult hippo drinks. It turned out to be 200 litres of water in a 24-hour period. Sadly, we didn't have enough money to build Happy his own pan. Although he did get sunburnt and at one stage looked terribly dehydrated, as an adult bull, his skin was much tougher than that of a young animal and he survived – younger hippos wouldn't have done so without water in which to submerge. Other animals also benefited from the drinking troughs, which were virtually the only source of water during this searing drought.

The pan-building and pipe-laying was supported by Care for the Wild International, an English animal charity. After we had used a chunk of Jean-Roger's savings, I managed to raise funds within Zimbabwe to continue the feeding programme. With time I had more international support than local. The drought took its toll within Zimbabwe and so I had to write to as many people as I could think of to help; most of them were overseas.

In three decades I have fed emergency rations five times, so it's not as though I am feeding every year. The longest period I have had to feed was for 13 months when the rains didn't come and the drought was horrendous. Had I not done this there would not have been one hippo left. On average I have had to feed for about nine to ten months. It's an intensive operation and very hard work, but it's so worth it when you see live animals eating, and not starving to death. Luckily, the Turgwe Hippo Trust supporters are always very generous at times like this, and it's their donations that enable us to save the animals.

When the land invasions began in 2000, poaching became – and remains to this day – very much part of our daily lives. During those horrendous initial days of the invasions, our lives were threatened regularly by people supposedly come to reclaim land but who, in truth, were in the Conservancy to poach the wildlife. Although my work is predominantly for the protection of the hippos, many other animals live here too. So, in order to protect as many wild animals as we possibly could, I started feeding any animal that came along to the house. Our property is not fenced and so every wild animal can choose to move through or into our 'back yard' and, over time, some have become permanent members of our animal family.

With poachers about, the baboons and monkeys started feeling safer living nearer to us. There are many different family units in a baboon's extended family, and the more dominant family members have exclusive access to the large riverine trees around our property. It appears that there are 'class systems' not only in humans and other primates, but in all animal species: some are born to positions at the top of the herd, troop, pod or pack, and others are born, and remain, subservient. Dominant baboon males have their own specific females, and their offspring are born into, and remain part of, this top-ranking family. The less dominant baboons have to find trees further afield, and the same applies to their food; these baboons and their offspring remain subservient for their entire lives.

We now have over 70 chacma baboons that spend some of the daylight hours with us and at night roost in the riverine trees surrounding our home. They are joined by their cousins, the delicate-looking vervet monkeys, with over 35 of them coming along each day. Once the baboons and monkeys moved to our home, other animals followed. In time, even kudu and impala would venture into our open back yard during the day or night. To encourage them all to stay during those bad years of violence and really heavy poaching I would lay out horse cubes and this has become a regular treat. Our home now is very much part of all of these wild animals' daily or nightly route through the bush and has become a haven for so many creatures.

We have over 40 warthogs that have chosen to live 'with' us, setting up at night in underground burrows relatively close to our home. Poachers hunt warthogs by setting fires around several exit points of their burrow, leaving just one hole open. The warthogs, in a panic, rush out of this one exit, where the poachers and their hunting dogs are waiting. If the dogs grab a warthog, the poachers will then often cut at the legs of the animal with a machete, thus hamstringing it and causing it to fall. An entire family of warthogs can all be caught and killed in this manner. By having the warthogs live closer to us, we are able to protect them a lot better: we can hear any dogs brought into our area as they bark when they locate the scent of an animal.

Our nearest neighbours live some 19 kilometres away, so we do live a rather isolated life, with hardly any intervention from humans. But we are content living in the wild, surrounded by lions, elephants, buffalos and, of course, hippos. And all of these animals get titbits.

Perhaps the most exciting thing about living in the bush with Nature is that almost every day can hold a surprise, a new revelation or just something to bring about a smile.

3

Kuchek hippo

In all my years working with these hippos I have not encountered a young male allowed to stay with his family, with just one exception, and that is Kuchek.

One day we got word of a problem mother hippo and her son living at a dam about four hours' drive away from us. She and her son had moved to the dam, possibly after leaving a nearby river system. Sadly, they had then become crop raiders, eating the produce grown by local communities. So National Parks rangers had been summoned by the chairman of the local village and told to shoot both hippos. Once animals get tagged with the label 'problem animal' they are usually killed, and the villagers are given the meat.

Luckily for these two hippos, Mike, the Wildlife Society chairman in the nearest town, heard about their predicament. He contacted me and asked if we would be prepared to foot the bill to have them captured and brought down to our area to be released. If so, he would arrange everything regarding their capture. I was aware that I couldn't have them released into the Turgwe River, for the youngster was a male and would be killed by Bob, the dominant bull in our area, or at least attacked and badly hurt. I needed somewhere that they could be alone and in time find their own way to an area they liked. I approached Roger Whittall about bringing the two hippos onto his property, and he agreed. Roger chose for the hippos a natural pan about 35 kilometres away, close to his boundary with the Sabi River.

For several weeks Mike and a friend worked at encouraging the two hippos to enter a trailer that the wildlife capture company had placed near to the dam. They had put up an electric fence encircling the entire dam so that the only food available to the hippos was a little bit of grazing near the edge of the dam – and hay and horse cubes that they laid around and inside the trailer. They built a grass hide near the truck to sit behind, and they hoped to be able to drop the gate once the hippos were habituated to the situation and both inside. This all sounds quite easy but hippos, like all wild animals, are not used to entering man-made structures, even if there is food as bait inside.

Determined to succeed, the men waited patiently for the hippos to start entering and feeding inside the trailer, and getting accustomed to it, and after about three weeks they felt that the hippos were finally ready for entrapment. On top of the trailer was a steel drop gate that had a wire attached to it, and to their massive relief they managed to drop the gate, with both hippos – mother and son – securely inside the trailer.

A phone call to our neighbours, relayed to us by radio transmission as we did not have our own phone line, conveyed the message that the hippos had been captured. I had arranged with Roger Whittall that I, together with two of his employees, Cuan and Peter, would be ready to meet the hippos at a crossing called the Turgwe Drift, a cemented causeway across the river. The trailer containing two unimpressed hippos had by now been attached to the lorry we had hired, and was on its way down to the Lowveld.

A journey that should not have taken longer than four hours stretched to seven (the truck driver had taken a 'short cut' that turned into a much longer route), as we waited and waited for the call to let us know that the truck had come through the boom of the Conservancy at the northern boundary, 50 kilometres away. Fortunately, because it was night time, it was relatively cool for the hippos, and there was hardly any traffic on the roads.

At about 1 a.m. the radio came to life with the voice of the boom ranger letting us know the truck had just entered the Conservancy. I picked up Roger's two helpers and we went to the drift to wait for the lorry so we could direct it to the area Roger had chosen for the hippos. On the arrival of the truck we instructed the driver to follow us to the pan, which was another 15 kilometres further on, and we arrived at the hippos' release place at well past 2 a.m. Seven hours in the truck must have been traumatic for the animals but there was nothing we could do other than hope that they would settle happily in their new home.

The three of us climbed up the side of the lorry and, by peering over the top, we could just make out the two hippos below us. The female seemed relatively relaxed, but her son of around three years of age was very agitated and more than ready to get out of the trailer. He was throwing his head around and sweating quite a lot. It took Cuan and Pete a while to connect the main wire of the release gate, and then, by climbing right up on top, Cuan would be able to pull the gate up while Pete and I stood away from the door. The pan was right next to the truck, so I hoped the hippos would head for water and not make for open land. The driver and his mate were safely back inside the front of the truck as neither was keen to meet a hippo at close range.

Cuan pulled up the door and nothing happened. No hippos appeared! Were they too scared to leave? My mind raced, wondering how we would push two hippos out of a trailer to their new freedom. Cuan lightly tapped the top of the door, and being metal, it made quite a sound – and that was all that was needed. There was an explosion of movement as two hippos shot out of the trailer as if pursued by all the bad things they had ever encountered. They moved off at top speed in the direction of the pan and we could hardly make out their shapes in the dark. I did not want to shine a torch on them as this would possibly disturb them even more, so now all we could do was wait for an hour or so until I was certain they had moved well away from the truck. Then the driver could start up the engine again and we could all go home to our welcome beds. It had been a long night, but rewarding, as these two hippos would have a new chance of life and wouldn't automatically be shot.

The translocated pair chose to move away from the pan the following day, and for the next week I tracked them on my own, finding them moving into other pans close by. Then one day I found their tracks at a broken fence on the edge of Roger's property heading off towards the Sabi River. I had not known about the fence being down and somehow the hippos had found it. I was really worried as the Sabi borders a huge communal area. With thousands of people settled on the opposite bank of the river, I feared that the hippos might head across and raid the community's crops.

Thankfully, one of Roger's excellent African trackers, Ndapo, managed to follow their tracks and we found them four days later back in the Turgwe, right at the boundary of the Turgwe and Sabi rivers, and there they remained for the next year.

Then, much to my amazement, in 1999 the mother moved up the Turgwe River and arrived at the pool where Happy, the other dominant bull in the area, lived with his family one kilometre upstream of our home. I recognised her straightaway as she had a differently shaped head from those of the Turgwe hippos: it was much squarer, with more hair visible around her ears and eyebrows, and she was generally a more hairy hippo than the others. At first, as is the way with hippos, the other females were extremely aggressive towards her, but she had no intention of leaving for she had found a pool and a pod. Happy the bull protected her from the start, staying close to her, and after a few months the rest of the hippos accepted her into the bloat.

Her son didn't ever arrive, so I had to assume that, as a male, he had to move off on his own. His mother must have waited to settle him in his own habitat before she moved to Happy's pool, following the river down to us, a journey of over 20 kilometres. I named her Mystery, for I knew nothing about her past or her breeding, and in March 2001 she gave birth to Kuchek, a son for Happy and her first calf born in the Turgwe River.

The two dominant bulls in the area occupied different areas: while Happy and his pod lived upstream from our home, moving at night to graze on a property called Angus, Robin and his pod lived downstream, grazing in our area and on Chlabata and Chigwete lands. So each had their own family and kept away from the other bull's territory. It is the female hippos that go looking for the bulls and, when Kuchek was two years old, Mystery left Happy's family and moved with her calf to join Robin's pod. Mystery's calf was likely accepted by Robin because of his young age.

Robin had a deformed front foot, probably caused by a bad injury in the past. The foot turned slightly to one side, so his gait on land was not as fast as that of most hippos and he left a track in the sand that made it easy to identify him. He did not seem unduly affected by the foot, so it likely happened when he was young, but it's possible that it made him less steady, and hence vulnerable to any other large bull that might challenge him, particularly on land. But at that time he and Happy kept their distance from each other.

In due course Mystery gave birth to another male calf, whom I named Zen. As most mother hippos will do, she attacked her older son Kuchek to keep him away from his young brother. But unlike all the others that I had studied, she stopped short of chasing him away from the pod, and nor did Robin intervene. Instead, Kuchek tolerated his mother's aggression and stayed with his family. I would daily witness Mystery chasing and attacking him whenever he came too close, but he remained in the pool and learnt to stay away from her. Finally, she seemed to lose interest in him. And then, to my surprise, he became Robin's close companion. This was unusual and I put it down to Robin's wonky foot and perhaps liking having a younger male with him in case some challenger were to return. Such a confrontation would inevitably one day take place (see chapter 20, Tembia hippo).

4

Understanding hippos

Although I am not scientifically trained, I have managed over the years to work out simple ways to study wildlife and to record every tiny thing I have learned. This has paved the way for my three decades of knowledge about hippos, and formed my understanding of this misunderstood and much maligned animal.

The Turgwe hippos were unlike those I had known when I worked as a safari guide. Those hippos had been living mainly in National Parks, where their protection was paramount. In our area hippos had been on the trophy list for sport hunting by our neighbours. Roger Whittall runs sport hunting as one of his main businesses as well as his cattle ranching; and the people who owned a huge tract of land on the other side of the Turgwe River, under the auspices of a ranch called Devuli, also sport hunted.

Hippos have their own hierarchical system, with a dominant bull in charge. The bull is surrounded by his family of females and calves and, occasionally, a juvenile male or two. His family, or bloat, generally numbers up to about 15 members. Female offspring tend to remain with the family, but males have to leave at a very early age, often as young as two-and-a-half years, when they have only just stopped suckling from their mother. I have also recorded juvenile hippos suckling up until around three-and-a-half years old, but that's if their mother is not pregnant again and allows them to drink. Once she is pregnant she often weans her son in a most aggressive manner, attacking him and even injuring him if he refuses to move away from her side. Young females also get harassed, but not normally chased out of the family.

Young males that are evicted from the bloat will move far away looking for a new pool in which to live, and in due course to start their own bloat. Males in larger river systems can often stay closer to the family as there is enough space for them to set up a new family unit relatively nearby, and to get away if conflict arises.

There were two dominant bulls in the area when we moved in. I had named one Happy thanks to his gentle disposition, and the other was called Bob, named by Patrick who worked with us at the bush camp.

Happy lived just upstream from our camp with his own family, while Bob was about two kilometres downstream with his females and calves. The two hippos were very different in behaviour and character. Happy was quite timid and kept a low profile, whilst Bob was often extremely aggressive towards me or, for that matter, any human being. He would mock charge if anyone got too close to the river's edge, and often left the water to follow up his charge. This really puzzled me as I had only seen that kind of behaviour in females with young calves – like all mothers, they are extremely protective of their babies. Bob and a mature female in his harem, whom I named Blackface, were not in any way calm when I was near the river.

For the first couple of years I found myself at times having to run for my life and quickly climb a tree. Blackface would regularly give perhaps one warning snort of anger, and the next second she would be out of the river and coming right after me at full speed. I was very aware of her and what mood she was in and, luckily, on each occasion I managed to extract myself in time, either getting away on foot or climbing the nearest tree. I always looked out for suitable trees when I approached the hippos' pools.

I had never come across such aggression before, and was determined to find out why these particular hippos behaved like this. My theory was that if I did not harass them then, with time, they would become used to me. It was clear, however, that the scent or sight of me always got the two of them agitated, and the situation was not obviously improving. But by watching them from a distance and listening to their constant 'conversation', I hit upon an idea. Why not talk to them? Not just 'hi guys' but rather keep up a constant monologue, getting them to recognise and become used to my voice.

Slowly this began to work. Before approaching the riverbank I would start calling their names and just chatting away to all of the family. It took nearly three years of my talking for Bob to calm down; and when he did, it was to such an extent that we eventually developed the most amazing bond. I would call his name, and even if he was far up or downstream from his pool, I would suddenly see a tidal wave approaching and every now and then the snout of a large hippo would appear above the surface, take a breath and drop below the water again as he propelled himself along the river bottom straight in my direction. Then, perhaps seven metres from where I was standing, an immense explosion of water would be sent rocketing up into the sky. Out of that massive spray would pop Bob, his huge head and all of his body coming up above the surface – driven not by anger and fear, as in the early days, but by way of greeting me.

Living with hippos and spending hours each day watching them, I was learning so much more than when I had been working as a guide. The eyes and ears of a hippo can tell you much about them. If their eyes are tight and their ears held back a bit then, as with many other animals, this is a sign of anger or sometimes fear. Ears flicking and in the forward position, as in a horse, and a softness in the eyes show acceptance. When calves play and engage in games in the river such as jumping over each other, looking more like little dolphins, or begin their open-mouthed pushing games, the expressions on their faces and their body language show clearly that they are having fun.

That hippos are intelligent and can learn to understand humans is not something most people even consider. However, as my hippos grew accustomed to me and gradually relaxed their guard in my presence, it seemed to free up their other senses, both in terms of expressing themselves and in listening to me.

In 32 years I have had to feed the hippos for five periods during extreme droughts. Kuchek, who was born in March 2001, has been fed by me four times, three of those periods when he had his own family. Silas and I would be laying out the food, consisting of bales of hay with a mixture of horse cubes and survival ration, at the feeding station situated just below our house. Kuchek would always be one of the first hippos to arrive, and then his family would follow a few minutes after him. Sometimes we had not yet finished laying out the food, and so I would say to Kuchek in a strong voice, 'Kuchek, wait!' Astonishingly, this massive animal would look at me, then look at his food and obediently stop in his tracks, often resting his heavy head on a rock while we finished mixing the food and getting it ready for them all. If he got slightly impatient and showed that he might be wanting to start eating, I would once more ask him to wait, and sure enough, he would. As soon as we had finished putting out all the food we would start walking away. I would then say to Kuch, 'OK, boy, you can come now. Come on, Kuchy', and with that he would be on his way to the food. We could be just a few metres away, but he just headed to his food and promptly started feeding. This was just so amazing, it's beyond words; by listening to me he paid me the greatest honour.

Kuchek knew exactly what was happening and he understood what I was saying. I believe that all animals understand us; it is we who do not understand them. When you treat animals with respect, you earn their trust, and the special bonding moments I have had with wild hippos in their own habitat will stay with me for the rest of my life.

One of the things I learnt more about through direct experience with the Turgwe hippos was something I had always known about, but not fully understood: that hippos secrete a kind of gel that's red and looks a lot like blood, giving rise to the idea that hippos 'sweat blood'. In later years, when Steve first came to the house (see chapter 16, Steve hippo) with this red gel coming from his legs and face area I really thought he was bleeding. I had seen this discharge on hippos in the river, but to see it up close and be able to touch it was novel. It would drip down from his body onto the cemented ground near our back door. Once Steve had moved off I would go outside and collect a bit of the gel. It had the consistency of a moisturising cream and when rubbed into my skin it soaked in quickly, leaving my skin feeling so soft and looking, I believe, less wrinkled! He has always secreted this kind of liquid whenever stressed or encountering something unusual: if Kuchek had harassed him, or if the river had come down in a freak flood and he'd had to get out quickly and move to a quieter spot, the discharge was noticeable. Research has shown that the gel has antibacterial properties and may also act as a sunscreen. Although it's not strictly sweat, it could also play a similar role to that of conventional sweat in helping to control hippos' body temperature. Knowing this was another way for me to understand and gauge the wellbeing of my hippos, thanks to Stevie's visits to our back door.

5

Life in the bush

I came to Africa as a young girl, trusting that if we all worked for a common cause – the conservation of animals – we would be like one big family, a team of like-minded people who would put kindness and compassion first. That girl very quickly had such ideas knocked out of her. Over the years and considering the experiences I have had, my eyes have been well and truly opened and my heart has, I am sure, slowly hardened. I do not like the word 'conservation'. It is used far too lightly by many whose agenda has nothing to do with preserving the life of sentient beings, but everything to do with the management and control of wildlife.

Jean-Roger was, when I first met him, more academic and theoretical than practical. His father Franco had started life in the building trade, working his way up into management, which was a huge achievement for an Italian immigrant to France. Franco and his wife had made sure that their four children had a good education, giving them the best chance in life. Jean had qualified top of his final year in geology and, with his ability to speak seven languages and his pilot's licence, he was assured of a bright future.

Franco was immensely proud of all of his children, but it was his first-born, Jean-Roger, who took the brunt of his father's strict discipline. Franco made sure that Jean, as a young boy, worked on construction sites, just to have another skill under his belt. From the age of 15, Jean was required to carry, climb and fetch with the building team every school holiday. They lived in the French Alps where temperatures can plummet to well below freezing in the winter, but work had to carry on regardless.

Jean hated the enforced manual work and suffered from a fear of heights, particularly when he had to climb scaffolding or balance precariously on a high building platform. But he was later to find that the knowledge he had gained as a youth would really come into play here in the African bush. This was especially so when, after we had lived under canvas for three years, he set about building our house. He was helped by just me and one local man, whom Jean taught to build with rocks and other natural materials. The three of us built our home.

I was the main designer, both exterior and interior, although some of my less practical ideas were shot down in flames. The house has a view down to the river, and as far as one can see there is bush, with forests of mopane trees and rock koppies in the distance. The walls are built partly of rocks, each of which had to be carried down from the koppies by wheelbarrow; and partly of bricks, locally made and fired in a kiln inside a disused anthill. We have plastered some of the brick walls and are able to hang the odd photo. The kitchen and bathroom have all-brick walls and an asbestos roof, with a ceiling made from local matting; the rest of the house is entirely thatched. Thatching was the only aspect of the house that required professionals and we hired a team from Bulawayo, where the best thatching grass is found. We also had to hire a 15-ton truck to transport the grass.

The early years were particularly hard. Jean-Roger was away working, so I would just have to wait for him to come home at the end of the month to fill him in about all the dramas that had occurred in his absence. At that stage in our lives, in the late 1990s, he was at home for only one week a month as his work took him all around Zimbabwe and he lived wherever the work took him. I lived alone with the animals and, although our neighbours were far away, I so loved my life with the hippos that loneliness never bothered me.

It was much harder on Jean-Roger. Working in mining exploration most of the time, he was either out in the bush, sleeping at night in a tent, or in the company's small caravan, which he really did not enjoy. But one of us had to earn an income. The Turgwe Hippo

Trust was my creation and so I was not paid a salary. My main focus has always been the hippos and the other animals; all funding to the Trust goes straight back into the daily running costs and projects for the animals.

In order to raise funds for the Trust we decided in 1999 to take in paying volunteers – an acknowledged method of support among outfits such as ours. The donation each volunteer gave during our relatively peaceful times really helped to keep everything going. However, during the bad years of land invasions from 2000 until 2007 it wouldn't have been safe to have people stay with us. This meant a very lean period for the Trust as I had to raise funds for all the monthly expenses. And in 2008 we decided, with relief, that it was safe enough to start having volunteers again.

Our volunteers usually end up not doing much work physically during their 10-day stay, but rather enjoying what is for them a very novel lifestyle. They help with all the wildlife that comes to the house, putting out food, as well as accompanying me on my daily routines: walking in the bush, climbing koppies for a better view, keeping a lookout for tracks of people and looking for snares. We spend a lot of time with the hippos if they are in areas where it's easy to watch them. I also drive into other areas to show them the wildlife. They have cottages to stay in but, apart from this relatively nice accommodation, they get to experience the life that we have led for all these years. We even do all the cooking for them, so they have a somewhat luxurious time with us, but the best thing is their exposure to all the wildlife in our unfenced property.

Newcomers soon come face to face with the realities of living in the bush. Having spent two weeks with us, a lovely Hungarian girl called Orsi revealed that what – from the outside – looked like paradise to anyone keen to visit Africa, was proving not to be the case. She was amazed at how many of the everyday things she took for granted in Hungary were for us quite complex, and often took time and involved hard work.

She, like all our volunteers, was to learn that malaria is still rampant and kills many people; that life and death situations can pop up quite regularly in the bush, often caused by something tiny like a mosquito, spider or a scorpion; and that you often take your life in your hands when using public transport, such as an overcrowded bus. It soon became apparent that even if you drive yourself you have to watch out for other drivers, children, cattle and goats, and often travel on roads that have more potholes than driving surface.

It surprised some volunteers that at our home, an ordinary facility like clean drinking water from a tap doesn't exist. Initially we would pump our water from the deep borehole and piping setup of the Whittalls, who live 19 kilometres away. Even now we still collect our drinking water from their borehole, and it is probably the purest water in Zimbabwe. Five 20-litre containers last us about a week if we don't have any visitors. We could drink the river water, but bilharzia is another African disease that you do not want to get, and filtering such water for drinking is not advised. For washing, we pump water from the river and treat it with chlorine in our storage tanks.

Our hot-water setup consists of a 200-litre drum that lies horizontally on a metal grid, surrounded on three sides by a brick wall. Water is pumped into the drum; then, using dead dry wood collected in the bush, a fire is made under the grid, heating up the water in the drum. The hot water is pumped out through pipes leading to our homestead and to the volunteer cottages. One snag is that 200 litres is relatively little hot water, so this is another commodity that's never taken for granted.

For many years we had very limited access to the outside world, even after the global advent of the internet. However, after years of climbing the nearest koppie carrying our laptop and then getting a signal with the cell phone from the highest point of the rocky hill, we now have our own wi-fi setup and can correspond with the world. We have a satellite dish that works once the generator is turned on, although we are probably the only people in Zimbabwe whose dish is in a cage to discourage the baboons and monkeys from swinging on and dislodging it.

If you want a social life then the bush is not for you. We go to the city of Harare maybe three times a year, a drive of over 450 kilometres one way, taking six to seven hours on roads that are poor in places. We spend most of the year here, at Hippo Haven, and in the first years the only people we saw were those who came to visit the hippos. However, in our time here we have made many new 'virtual' friends, often people who have initially contacted me through their interest in hippos, and we have eventually met some of them in person. We have also met people overseas who have then come here to volunteer with us. Nowadays we have many international volunteers and quite a few have become good friends. Although they often live very far away, across the ocean, we can at least enjoy their virtual company and even occasional visits.

Most of the people living around this area practise sport hunting and believe in the sustainable use of animals, making a business out of the wildlife and utilising it to the full. I call it 'farming wildlife'. By contrast, I run a charity not just for the hippos, but also for all the other animals that have come into our lives, and our policy is to protect each and every one of them. Neither of us agrees with any kind of sustainable use of an animal if it involves the animal's death at the end of the journey.

Luckily, there are a few people relatively nearby with whom we do have things in common. They live about 50 kilometres away in the north of this Conservancy and are also in no way connected with killing animals in order to make a living. Bryce and Lara Clemence are there to protect the endangered rhinos, often putting their own lives on the line. South Africans Kim and Saskia Wolhuter make their living from filming animals. There is always a moral purpose to the filming, in Kim's case to show how another maligned animal, the hyena, is not deserving of its negative reputation. These animals, like hippos, are in no way the villains they are so often made out to be. So at least every now and then we have human companionship, people that we feel are our friends.

If one is delicate or constantly in need of company, then this is really not the place to live. But for us, the scarcity of compatible human companionship is more than compensated for by the excitement of daily challenges. Although Jean-Roger doesn't feel the same intense passion about the hippos or the other animals, he does, however, love his life here in the bush. For me, living in the company of so many animals is the realisation of my dreams. The Turgwe Hippo Trust is my creation and has given me a purpose in life, one that I do not take lightly. I am prepared to sacrifice everything for the future of the hippos.

6

Rescued animals

Living in the bush teaches one to become extremely self-sufficient as well as highly versatile. Unlike in an urban setting, there is no-one to call for help if you have a problem. Be it mechanical, practical, medical or almost anything else, you have to use your own common sense. As they say in Zimbabwe, 'make a plan' and somehow find a way to make it work.

Early one morning Jean-Roger and I were out walking, patrolling for signs of poachers or the snares that they set to trap animals. We were following the tracks of the rangers who work for us, as we like to check that they have taken the routes we wanted them to follow, and see for ourselves if there are any signs of poaching in the area. Poachers always leave tracks, be it full shoe footprints or other spoor left by someone walking in their socks or on their toes, usually on soft sand or mud. We know the tracks left by our rangers' boots, so any other tracks would be made by unwanted visitors.

Poaching in our area is not just 'hunting for the pot' – it's organised crime. The areas to the south and east of us were taken over in 2001 by people sent by the government to invade land, to take it away from the people who owned it, or to move in and harass the owners. Their main purpose, however, was to poach the wild animals and sell the meat commercially. They used carts drawn by oxen to carry out loads of dead animals to the neighbouring communities. The meat was sold to middle men, who transported it to the cities, or it was ordered by rich government-connected officials who owned butcheries, so it was very big business in every way. After five years of just the two of us spending up to seven hours a day removing wire snares, it was becoming harder to keep on top of the deteriorating situation. It finally became so bad during the early 2000s that the Trust had to employ rangers – initially two, and today we have six permanent rangers.

One day on our regular patrol, Jean and I were walking along in single file, as usual – I tend to lead as Jean, having bad tinnitus, is a bit deaf – when I noticed an animal lying ahead of us. It appeared to be thrashing about, but did not seem able to get up. As we closed in on it we realised it was a young waterbuck calf; she couldn't stand up and, though she was kicking her legs frantically, she appeared to be paralysed in her hindquarters. There was no other sign of waterbuck, so we approached her, not sure if she had been hurt by a snake or a predator. There was no visible sign of a wound or blood, and she was not frothing at the mouth or rolling her eyes; she just couldn't get up.

We decided to try to help her into a standing position as she was small enough for the two of us to lift. As Jean bent down to try to steady her I heard a noise directly ahead of us and, to my alarm, I saw a large female waterbuck coming at us at full gallop. Within seconds she was in front of Jean and rising up on her hind legs, about to crash down with her front legs, thrusting the weight of her entire body on to his bent back. I had just enough time to give him a shove – luckily, because he was balancing precariously, he fell to one side. The waterbuck came down with a thud, just missing Jean's back. Had she landed on him, she could have broken his spine. Jean immediately realised what was going on and was up and running in seconds, as was I. She was one very angry waterbuck. Fortunately for us, she didn't follow, but instead she stood by her calf, desperately trying to help it. We knew there was no way we could assist her.

As a former safari guide I am very aware of the different behaviours of the cats, elephants, buffalos and hippos, but I didn't know that a waterbuck would behave in such a manner. I had underestimated the power of a mother's protective instinct. There was nothing we could do but move off. To be honest, both of us were pretty shaken up as she really could have hurt Jean very badly, so we decided to carry on with the patrol and then retrace our steps and see if the calf was still there on our return.

Two hours later we were back, but there was no sign of the baby or the mother, for that matter. I wondered if the calf could have been having a kind of epileptic fit, but I was not sure if waterbuck could be subject to such a thing. If it had been a snakebite, the calf wouldn't have survived as only a very venomous snake would have caused such a fit. We were flummoxed, but pleased that it appeared that the calf was now okay.

The next morning the rangers went off for their patrol and were back after a short time to give us the sad news that they had found a leopard kill. There was not much of the victim left, but enough to identify it as a calf and it seemed highly unlikely that it wasn't the baby waterbuck. Whatever was wrong with that calf had worked to the leopard's advantage. The rangers saw no sign of the mother so she must in the end have left her baby to the predator.

Happenings like this leave an emptiness in your stomach and a sadness that takes a few days to shift, but I have to tell myself that the death was natural, that the calf was most likely a weakling and that the leopard had also to survive. Nature feeds its own. I can handle this; it is when humans kill for nothing more than money or when they kill for pleasure and give it the name of 'sport' that I cannot accept it at all.

The following afternoon it seemed that fate was offering us an uplifting moment to take away the sadness we felt about the baby waterbuck. Jean and I had gone to see the hippos at one of the pools used by Kuchek's family. We arrived to see all nine hippos resting up against a large rock with two of their calves, Darrow and George. The calves were playing open-mouthed pushing games. Hippos do this for play, but later in their lives it's often a means of defence or rivalry, either two bulls vying for control of a bloat or, in the case of females, sorting out who is the more dominant cow.

As we watched, Jean suddenly drew my attention to a movement in the main channel of the Turgwe. The river was running quite strongly as the rains had arrived. The water was a dirty chocolate brown from the silt being washed downstream. In the turbulent waters a yellow spotted object caught my eye and I realised it was a large tortoise and it was being floated along by the current. It was desperately trying to keep its head up so as not to drown. There is an opening in the river bank that's used by the hippos to leave the river at dusk when they set off to graze. Jean quickly moved to this opening and lay down with his arms outstretched, hoping he might be able to grab the tortoise when it passed by – but it was just that bit too far away. He asked me to find a long branch with which he might be able to fish the tortoise towards him, but then something incredible happened. The tortoise saw Jean's outstretched hand and began swimming as much as it could towards him; it seemed to know that Jean wanted to save it.

As it reached his hand, the effort of swimming against the current was just too much and his head and neck, which had been outstretched above the water, flopped under the surface. Thankfully, right at that moment Jean managed to grab hold of the animal. It was a very big tortoise. We have two species here in the Lowveld and this one was the larger of the two, known as the leopard tortoise because of its yellow shell with dark spots. Jean dragged it to the bank and pulled it out. The poor thing was so exhausted that it couldn't move, but its head was out of the water and its eyes were bright. It was carrying a couple of very bloated live ticks which we promptly removed. We knew it was too tired to be left there as it would be ideal prey for some hungry predator, so we carried it home to spend the night in our bathroom, supplying it with water and some vegetables in case it was hungry.

The following morning we took the tortoise inland, away from the river, to an area where we knew there was a permanent natural pan with water and good grass, and yet far enough away from the regular routes of the poachers who would catch and eat a tortoise if they found one. So we lost the waterbuck but saved the tortoise, which made everything feel so much better.

On another occasion Yogi, a very large male baboon, came into the homestead carrying a poacher's wire snare. It was tightly attached to his lower body, cutting into his genitals and, if not removed, it would ultimately kill him. I managed to contact a colleague in the north of the Conservancy, Dr Rosemary Groom, who has a PhD in zoology and works with painted wild dogs. She is extremely good at what she does and has a drugs licence, so she would be able to shoot a tranquilliser and we would, hopefully, be able to remove the snare embedded in Yogi's torso.

It would be my job to find somewhere to restrain him until Rosemary could drive the hour-and-a-half journey on a bad dirt track from her home. I decided the best way would be to try to coax him into the fenced garage. So, using apples and an orange, which baboons adore, and by choosing a time when there were only a couple of his females around, I managed to get him to follow me into the caged garage.

I put the food on the ground and then left, shutting the wire gate. He looked at me, but did not in any way seem stressed, and promptly sat down and ate his fruit. I radioed Rosemary and told her he was caged but, to my dismay, she told me she couldn't come as something had cropped up with her own work. She asked me if I could try again the next day. I was terribly apprehensive that Yogi would panic, or that he wouldn't come to the house the next day, and that we wouldn't be able to remove the snare. But I feel that animals know when you are trying to help them, even wild animals. So I opened the door and he strolled out as if being locked in a wire cage happened to him every day. Though the snare was biting into his balls he could still walk, but you could see it was deep into his stomach area as well. This would eventually stop him from being able to eat properly.

The following day it all went like clockwork. Once more Yogi joined me in the garage. As a reward I gave him a bucket of horse cubes to keep him busy and happy. Rosemary was on her way so now all we had to do was wait. She and her colleague, Jessica, arrived and it was time to try to dart Yogi. It looked as though it should be relatively simple, although there was apprehension on my part as some animals have an adverse reaction to being drugged; I hoped he wouldn't be one of them. The drug is in a vial in the dart and Rosemary had to shoot the dart gun projectile through the large holes in the wire that enclosed the garage.

I talked to Yogi as she took aim, and boof, off went the dart straight into his side and, within a very short time, he was staggering around and then slowly he collapsed to the ground. We entered the garage with me going first, as naturally Rosemary and Jess were very aware of the reputation of baboons – and Yogi was a large male with huge teeth. Nobody need have worried as he was completely unconscious. The first job was to cover his eyes to protect them from drying out and then get to the important part of cutting off the wire. It was deeply embedded into his stomach area, but fortunately had not penetrated the lining or cut into his intestines. His genitals were also rather squashed, but again were not bleeding – he can't have been carrying the snare for too long. I just wondered how he had managed to break the wire and get away from the area where the snare was set. Thanks to his intelligence and immense strength he had taken a first step towards saving his life, but had we not been able to remove the snare it would still have killed him: it was deeply embedded, probably as a result of his struggle to free himself.

Once the wire was cut away, Rosemary and Jessica cleaned the wound, spraying it with gentian violet and giving him a jab of a quick-acting antibiotic. They told me it should take him an hour or so to wake and be fully mobile again, so it was best to keep him in the garage until he could move around normally. The other males and the entire troop were by now all in the vicinity and paying close attention to what we were up to. At one point I was worried they were going to try to get at him in the garage, as one of the traits of baboons is that they can be exceedingly jealous. If they thought he was getting preferential treatment they might try to intervene.

Maybe I didn't give them enough credit for their sensitivity as all of them were just hanging around watching, but without any form of threat or excitement. So, after thanking Rosemary and Jess profusely, I went back into the garage and joined Yogi to wait for him to wake up. Once he was sitting in an upright position and looking more alert I opened the gate and then sat outside and waited for him to be ready to walk out. Eventually, after another hour or so, he did just that, but the amazing thing was that he seemed to want to have closer contact with me. This was something he had never done before.

I fetched him one of our apples, cutting it into slices, and handed him a piece. I didn't expect him to take it physically – I would usually have to throw food towards him – but no, he not only took a slice from me but then he put it in his mouth and took hold of my hand and for seconds I found myself holding hands with a baboon.

I really believe that Yogi knew exactly what he was doing when he held my hand: he was thanking me for removing that snare. Proof to me was that, for the next several months, Yogi became my shadow. I could be walking in the bush alone when suddenly he would appear and accompany me on my walk, often walking either directly behind or next to me. He never held my hand again, but his constant companionship was a privilege. Eventually, he started hanging out with another troop of baboons that doesn't come near the house as the resident local troop will not let them.

If I came upon the troop they would all run away, which is normal baboon behaviour – except for my Yogi. He would stay with me for a time and then move off after his mates. Then he stopped appearing and I have never seen him again. He was always very much of an outsider in our home troop, so I think when he found acceptance by a new troop he moved with them when they decided to leave our area.

It was painful not to see him any more, but I have always told myself that if animals choose to stay with us it's a gift that they offer. And when they move on to live in another area or with their own kind somewhere else, then I must be satisfied that, for some part of their lives, they have lived with and befriended a human being, and given immense joy.

7

The arrival of a mongoose

On the 10ᵗʰ March 2013 a very special event occurred in our lives. On returning one afternoon from a four-kilometre walk in the bush I noticed in the distance a young tree that I couldn't identify. As I approached it to investigate what species it was I heard a high-pitched, squeaking cry that seemed to be coming from a fallen log, and that increased in volume the closer I came – and there, lying against the log, was a really small brown animal. One of its eyes was open and its umbilical cord was still attached; and it was wriggling and crying with all its might. The shrill squeaking noise was extraordinary, considering how tiny the animal was. At first I thought it might be a baby squirrel, but then I realised it was more than likely a baby mongoose, perhaps a dwarf mongoose. There was nothing to indicate where it had come from and it certainly couldn't walk; it was only able to wriggle and squeak. There was no hole in the log out of which it might have fallen and all I could think was that perhaps the mother had been carrying it in her mouth, as a cat does a kitten, and had been taken by a raptor, or that she had left it there for some other reason; maybe it was an unwanted runt.

I knew I couldn't leave it there alone as it was quite defenceless and, with the noise it was making, predators could easily find it. So I gently picked it up and carried it home. It was so tiny that it fitted into the palm of my hand. Once home, I decided the best thing to do was to put the little creature in cotton wool inside a small cardboard box and leave it in our pantry, where it would be safe from our pussycats.

Then I returned to the tree and set up my trail camera there. These battery-run cameras are sensitive to movement, so anything moving in their range is recorded. If mother mongoose came back, at least it would be worth returning the baby to this spot in the hope that she would then fetch it. In the meantime it needed warmth, safety and quiet, so the pantry seemed the best bet.

Jean was at home when I arrived back with the baby and he took one look at it and said, 'Karen, I hope you don't think you can rear that, it's far too young and tiny and there is no way it's going to make it. I see heartache and tears if you try.'

At times Jean can sound quite cold, but he has always been the practical one and he knows how much helping animals means to me. On the other hand, he usually takes the brunt of my pain if it doesn't work out. But I do not like to admit defeat so I turned on our generator in order to send an email to a colleague, Lisa Hywood, up in Harare.

Lisa runs the Tikki Hywood Foundation. She is an amazing woman who, in spite of many personal hardships, has created a setup for the rescue and release of a range of endangered wildlife species. Her work is mainly centred on the pangolin, but in the years she has been operating she has helped many other animals. She was the ideal person to speak to and she couldn't have been more kind or helpful.

Telling me exactly how to look after the baby, she said that it would need to be fed two-hourly with milk powder weighing 20 percent of its weight every feed. At that stage the tiny creature weighed 50 grams. The milk had to be blood heat, to be tested on the inside of one's wrist; and the baby had to have a hot-water bottle at all times, to be replaced every time it began to cool off. Lisa told me that if the baby made it, when we next drove up to Harare she could give us some feeding bottles as well as a little cage for her. She warned me that raising such a young mongoose would be very difficult and not to get too upset if it didn't make it. But at least I was now armed with essential information on how to proceed and give the little mongoose at least a chance of survival. I knew that it would only pass urine and poop once it had consumed enough liquid food, but also that, as with most baby animals, once they start feeding you have to rub their tiny bottoms with something moist, like a piece of cotton wool dipped in warm water. This stimulates their bowels and helps them to pee and poop, and is normally something their mothers do by licking their bottom. Even I couldn't contemplate such a service!

I went to check the camera a few hours later and found two photos that were entirely unexpected, given how close this was to our camp. Instead of what I had hoped for – an adult mongoose – there were two lions, both young males that had stopped right at the spot where the baby had been lying, had their photos taken and then moved on. The mongoose would have made for a nice hors d'oeuvre! I left the camera there for over a week, but the mother never did return.

I was afraid to name the baby as this would make it even more difficult for me if it didn't survive. But there's something sad about being nameless, so taking into account that she was still wriggling in her box and screaming, the name Squiggle popped into my head.

In order to feed her, Jean found some very thin rubber tubing used to repair bicycle tires that was soft and could be put onto a tiny syringe to form a rudimentary teat. We mixed a small amount of milk, heated to just the right temperature, and even though she was so tiny I still needed Jean to hold her while I fed her as she really could wriggle. I carefully pushed the soft tube inside the corner of her mouth and squirted in a drop of milk. We gave her not more than two or three drops and then put her back in her warm, cosy box alongside a hot-water bottle. We were now able to confirm that she was a female, something that became evident as I gently rubbed her bottom with damp cotton wool. Lisa had stressed that the most important thing was to feed her every two hours throughout the day and night, and that is how our lives were suddenly taken over for the next four weeks.

When such a small animal is so dependent, requiring constant care and attention, it's hard to gauge whether one is succeeding. But finally, on one of her feeds, a small squirt of urine with the tiniest of stools came out and we then knew we were making headway. Once her stools became a little larger I even took a photo of one and emailed it to Lisa. To this day we laugh about our pride over Squiggle's first proper poop.

41

Jean and I realised one thing about feeding babies: that sleep deprivation is not funny and it doesn't matter how old or young you are, breaking one's sleep pattern every two hours is seriously debilitating – even if in our case it was for only just over four weeks, for after that Squiggle could go through an entire night without a feed. Round-the-clock care for human babies doesn't stop at four weeks and so I can only salute human parents – they deserve medals!

When she was four weeks old it was time to introduce Squiggle to the other members of the household. By now she weighed about 200 grams and we had discovered that she was not a dwarf mongoose at all. The tip of her tail was turning black and so she was a slender mongoose. This turned out very well for all of us. Slenders are not clan mongooses and live a solitary life once they leave their mother, getting together with other mongooses only to mate. So Squiggle wouldn't be living an unusually lonely life for a mongoose; like us, she was an independent soul! At that stage I was still thinking she would eventually be released back into the wild, but we did not know then how a mongoose can worm its way into your world and into your very being.

As she became more confident we thought it safe to let her meet our pussycats, of which we had four in the house: three from my late mother and one of our own, Socks. I was terrified that they would see Squiggle as prey, viewing her as a mouse. But I think that, from the very first moment we let her wriggle around Socks and one of the smaller cats, they sensed that she was also a predator, and only one of the cats, Gama, showed much curiosity. Socks even appeared somewhat afraid of this squeaking, wobbly little creature, but then I have seen Socks run away from a mouse, so that kind of figured. Gama could be extremely fierce, but from day one she tolerated Squiggle's presence and it wasn't long before Squiggle would wriggle her way among the cats and bury herself in their fur, seeking warmth and comfort. They would just look her over and go back to sleep, or continue grooming themselves as if living with a mongoose was perfectly normal and acceptable. Of course, we did not leave her with them without one of us around; we always supervised any interaction, although we didn't ever pick up a look in the cats' eyes to suggest that mongoose could be on the menu.

Once Squiggle started lapping milk on her own she began to grow in leaps and bounds. Lisa had told me to weigh her daily and luckily we had a tiny cooking scale. At the time she fitted into a teacup, so this was the perfect vessel in which to weigh her. Soon she started to eat solids, first tiny slivers of cucumber, and then eggs. She preferred an egg scrambled in butter – and Squiggle got whatever she desired. But she also relished raw eggs, poached eggs and mealworms. These I had managed to get from a friend and, as they breed relatively quickly, I soon had plenty of worms living in a large bowl in the pantry to keep Squiggle happy between her mealtimes.

We discovered that she liked cheese, but we also tried to give her natural food like grasshoppers and the odd extra beetle larva. She ate what she liked and ignored things that did not appeal. Papaya and the odd piece of apple or avocado often caught her attention.

She had the most beautiful eyes. The iris was yellow and gold and the pupil black and slanted. She could also invert her eyelids, something that's done by many animals to protect their eyes. Her fur was a soft cuddly brownish-golden colour, sprinkled with tiny black and orange hairs, and she had the cutest, pinkest nose. I provided her with various items from my wardrobe for her to snuggle into. Her favourites were one of my knee-length pink woolly socks, into which she could burrow and completely disappear, and a fleece beanie that she would wrap around her tiny body and then peer out at the world, as if all mongooses lived inside beanie hats. She also loved one of my fluffy fleece jerseys.

I would carry her wherever I went in the house and she knew that this was home. She was walking by then, or should I say running, as Squiggle hardly ever walked anywhere; it was always a kind of gallop from one object to another, with her tail held up and the tip curled over, although when she was stationary her tail would stretch out behind her. She was endlessly inquisitive about whatever she could find in the house to play with or investigate. She loved the sewing box and would take everything out of it, and then roll around inside it herself. She had the longest toenails and she grew the sharpest teeth of probably any small predator. When she learnt she could bite she would playfully nip and we were staggered by the strength of her tiny jaws. In comparison to, say, a bulldog, her bite was harder and arguably hurt more. She would nip-and-run as if this was all part of an ongoing game with us.

Funnily enough, she hardly ever nipped me, but Jean became the main target of her fun and he thoroughly enjoyed it and encouraged her to play. She would launch herself at his body when he was, for example, making our bed, and she would attempt to bite at any part of his anatomy with her mouth agape, looking more like the shark in the movie *Jaws*, on a mission to give him a nip. A few times he found himself getting bitten in the balls by a mad mongoose, which he said was really not fun at all, and yet he still couldn't stop laughing. The more he laughed, the more angry Squiggy would become, and she would try to bite him again, often chasing him around the bed. My six-foot, well-built husband would find himself running away from a 500-gram mongoose and he would still be laughing as he ran out of the door. Squiggle was our boss in every way.

We Squiggle-proofed the house so that she couldn't get out, and would be safe in any room. We had built our house with a tiny gap above the walls where the thatch joined them, but with the arrival of Squiggle we had to cover all such gaps with mesh so that she couldn't escape – not that she wanted to. We were more afraid of her finding herself outside and not being able to get back in, or being attacked by one of our baboons or a raptor.

I have always been a very tidy person, but with the introduction of a mongoose into our home I became even more so. We had, as do parents of small children, to put away most of our things. Squiggle had a lovely habit of urinating on anything metallic: cell phones, plugs, laptops, mugs for tea ... we couldn't afford to keep replacing cell phones or laptops, so there was no option but to put them out of her reach if they were not being used.

Mongooses can climb as well as run fast, so you can imagine how very neat our home needed to be. Every night she came into bed with us, and after lying between us so I could stroke her soft fur for a while, she would snuggle down to the bottom of the bed and sleep next to my toes. She hated the cold, so on winter mornings she would often be the last one out of bed, and if it was a really cold day I had to bring her breakfast in bed. Squiggle really took over my life in every way.

What it meant to us as a couple was that we couldn't leave the house without her. If we had to go up to Harare, which is a seven-hour drive, nearly two hours of that through the bush, she came with us. To begin with she would snuggle on my lap, but as she grew and became more active it was safer for her to travel in a tiny cage. We always had to pack more things for our minute predator than for the two of us combined: her blankets, fluffy jerseys, dishes, food, toys and, of course, a very large cage (more suited to a medium-sized dog) in which she would live for the duration of our stay. We didn't ever travel with her for longer than three days as it was not fair for her to spend too long a period in a cage, when at home she had the run of the entire house as well as a large outside cage.

Once we were travelling up to Harare and Squig, who was still very tiny, was on my lap. She could move around fast, though. We had pulled off the road for me to take a pee, leaving Jean holding her until I returned. Suddenly she managed to slip away from him and disappear inside the vehicle. I went into a panic as there are so many little places under seats or elsewhere that a very small mongoose could hide. We closed the doors and windows and then began searching for her. At one stage I was more or less sitting on top of Jean with my skirt riding up as I searched under his seat without opening a door, just in case she managed to get out in the middle of nowhere. The windows by then were pretty steamed-up, when suddenly I saw an African a man peering at me through the hazy glass. I can just imagine what he thought was going on in this parked car. We laughed a lot about it once we had Squiggle safely back on my lap, but I wonder if he went home and told his family about these people he'd caught getting up to no good in their car!

In the early days we were lucky to be able to stay with friends or colleagues up in Harare. One couple became accustomed to our travelling with animals. Years before Squiggle arrived I had a tortoise named Tony, who came with us wherever we went. Then there were often cats needing to see a vet, especially when my mum passed away and left me 11 elderly felines! Three of them, Gama, Tortie and Moxie, got to meet and live with Squiggle. When we couldn't stay with people that we knew, and who were prepared also to accommodate Squiggle, we would smuggle her into a guest house or small lodge, lock the bathroom door and take the key with us when we went out, although we usually ended up telling the owner of the establishment that we travelled with a mongoose.

Usually Squiggle had the run of the entire house as well as her outside cage, but we also built several other cages for her over time, each one bigger than the last for such a tiny little girl. To accommodate her while we were away, we built a *very* large cage, more suited to a small pony than a mongoose. Our trusted helper Silas would sleep in a bed alongside the cage, where he could keep an eye on her, although she would never allow him to handle her. We installed pipes in the cage for her to run through, and branches, and a sliding door so that Silas could top up her food and water without letting her out. I placed two drawers from an old desk in the cage, one on top of the other to form a sort of cave, with all her favourite woolly socks and jerseys to snuggle into inside the drawers. It was a pretty luxurious home, specially considering we only left her perhaps five times in an entire year, mainly for the two days when we took volunteers to the National Park. She was never happy when I put her in the cage, and I would certainly get 'the look' as I did so, but she would soon settle down.

We knew that at some stage we would have to take a proper break from our lives in the bush. However, we couldn't contemplate going away and leaving our mongoose for any time without a house sitter. The Turgwe Hippo Trust also required some form of oversight for it to continue functioning properly in our absence. With rangers in our employ and daily routines required for the animals, as well as recording of the hippos' lives and the work I had online, we needed somebody reliable, whom we could trust to take care of everything. One of the volunteers who came along to the Trust proved not only to be the perfect assistant for our work, but she also became the Trust's official house sitter when we took a long-term break. That Mirinda Thorpe would fly all the way from Australia to help us out proved her extraordinary dedication and value to us and to the Turgwe Hippo Trust.

When we started out, Jean-Roger and I were camped above the Turgwe River, living in a lean-to that we had made: an open-fronted canvas dwelling with corrugated iron sheets for the roof. We used the caravan as a kitchen and to keep our cats and cocker spaniel safe at night from predators.

After we had lived under canvas for three years, we set about building our house. We were assisted by a local man whom Jean-Roger taught to build using rocks and other natural materials. The house has a view down to the river, and as far as one can see there is bush, with forests of mopane trees and rock koppies in the distance.

During periods of severe drought, we source hay from Marondera, about 70 kilometres east of Harare, and it is transported to Hippo Haven, 500 kilometres away in south-eastern Zimbabwe. A one-way trip can take up to two days if the loading time is included.

During severe droughts our priority is to feed the hippos, but cabbages bought from nearby communities, if available, and excess hay are fed to other wildlife.

It's all hands on deck when the food trucks arrive, and volunteers and rangers all help to offload food as soon as it arrives.

This is one of three water pans we built for the hippos and other wildlife. The cemented pans, which are filled with river water, are a lifesaver during times of drought. We have laid pipelines to the house from the pans for use during normal times but when drought strikes we switch to using borehole water.

Kuchek, our resident dominant bull, shows off by gaping for the camera.

A much younger Kuchek takes a nap with a friend.

Here I am, with Kuchek to the left of Relief and Max behind her on land. In the distance, Tacha peers above the surface of the water. The hippos are completely accepting of me, even climbing up on the bank and lying down in front of me.

After raiding the crops in local communities, some four hours' drive away from us, Mystery and her younger son were classified 'problem animals' and thus destined to be shot. The Turgwe Hippo Trust agreed to have them captured and translocated, and the pair were settled on a nearby property. Months later, Mystery arrived at the Turgwe River and joined the family of hippos there. In 2000 she was mated by Happy, and Kuchek was born in March 2001.

Wildlife ecologist Dr Rosemary Groom (left), with the help of conservation biologist Jessica Watermeyer (right), darts Yogi to remove a poacher's wire snare embedded deep in his torso. Rosemary is the chief executive officer of the African Wildlife Conservation Fund and Jessica its projects director.

Yogi walked with me in the bush for a long time after his snare was removed.

The rangers patrol the bush every day looking for snares or poacher tracks. In 2023, over sixteen poachers were caught. Silas Matyarutsa (seated) is my right-hand man, doing things like making small bridges across the Turgwe River so that I can check on the hippos. He has worked with the Turgwe Hippo Trust for three decades – he can fix nearly anything. From left to right (standing) are Peter Mabasa, Derek Manyere, Elijah Mahlengezana, Alphonse Matekwe, Thomas Dandauta and Tapera Musevenzo.

Samples of the snares that the rangers, Jean-Roger and I have picked up in the bush. The poachers use them to trap wildlife.

Squiggle mongoose weighed only 50 grams when I first found her in March 2013.

As a baby, Squiggle was so tiny that she could fit into a tea cup.

Once Squiggle was bigger she was introduced to the house cats. Here she is cuddling up to my late mother's cat, Long Socks. Squiggle ended up living in the house with five cats: four from my late mother and one of our own.

Initially Squiggle required round-the-clock care, but luckily this lasted only about four weeks. By that time she had gained weight and was ready to meet the other members of the household.

8

Baboons

Some animals, such as baboons, hippos and hyenas, tend to have bad reputations. Baboons are not popular with farmers or, come to think of it, with people in general. One of the main reasons is that, being the intelligent animals that they are, baboons know how to steal with impunity. If you are the victim of a baboon raid on your crops or vegetable garden, or even your kitchen, you won't feel much compassion for them. Fortunately, baboons can live in many different types of habitat and those that are not near farming areas, homesteads, safari camps or hotels can usually live out their lives in relative peace – though their natural predators, such as leopards and raptors, including large owls, are ever-present threats.

They breed prolifically and troops of up to 100 animals are not uncommon in areas such as National Parks and places where they are not harassed by humans. In our area, before it was overrun by land invaders, we would see baboons in the bush, but they always kept very much to themselves. In 2001, when the land occupiers arrived and took over many stretches of land along the river, the baboons found themselves frequently attacked by catapult-wielding people. Or their roosting trees would be burnt to the ground, and many were killed by dogs belonging to the invaders.

This was when the baboons moved down to our home. We posed no threat to them and there were a lot of nice large trees below our house in the riverbed where they could roost at night. As violence from the invading people escalated in the 2000s we found that the baboons provided an early alarm system to warn us if what we called the 'bad guys' were approaching our home.

We discovered that baboons, like vervet monkeys, have their own verbalisation for every single predator out there in the bush, including for humans. Their calls for predators such as leopards, painted wild dogs, cheetahs and people are all subtly different, and the warning when lions are around is particularly recognisable. Because of their living in close proximity to us, and being present every evening as well as sometimes during the daylight hours, we soon learnt their language. This proved to be very useful during the years when groups of thuggish invaders were being verbally violent and threatening towards us, harassing us often on a daily basis. The baboons always warned us well in advance if a group of thugs was heading our way and, although they would never attack the invaders they may even have been seen by the visitors as a potentially dangerous 'security force'. The males can grow to an impressive size so that, when standing up on their back legs, they are nearly as tall as me (I am five foot four inches, or 1.63 metres tall). During those awfully violent and upsetting years when we had to call the police or meet with them in the nearest town, Chiredzi, or when we encountered them at a road block to check our vehicle, they would ask, 'How are your soldiers?', which was their name for the baboons that 'oversaw' our home security.

So from those bad years something good came about. Unlike most people who discourage baboons from living near their homesteads or settlements, we needed them and were happy to live with them – we are probably the only human beings who voluntarily live with wild baboons. We began to give them food supplementation, not because they needed it as there was still plenty of food to be had in the bush, but to keep them close to our home, and even to thank them.

There is a rigid hierarchy in baboon troops. There is always a dominant male (sometimes two), and ranked beneath him are his lieutenants. The females of the dominant male enjoy elevated status too, as do his babies. Babies born to subservient mothers will never rise up in the ranks, remaining subservient for the rest of their life. Males sometimes leave one troop and join another, and it's possible that they can then achieve higher status – but this is not known.

Baboons exhibit strong behaviour patterns. At dawn, the dominant local 'bosses' and their family leave their roosts in the trees around our house and come down to start their day. They first have a 'snack' – supplementary food that we supply – before setting off to forage in the bush. When they have departed, the lower-ranked baboons arrive for their supplementary food. Once the main troop is back they all do their own thing around the house as it's now very much part of their habitat. This relaxed proximity has allowed us to learn about baboons in a unique manner. They are altogether comfortable in the vicinity of the house and, if anything, we are the onlookers. Their behaviour is completely natural and we have become part of their lives, which is very special. They clearly feel that our home is their home, and we often find them sitting in our outside chairs in the gazebo, which is a very endearing sight.

Jean-Roger is very good at recognising different faces within the baboon family, which averaged around 30 individuals, and so he began to name many of the more prominent members. I can recognise all the hippos as they are my study animal but, unlike Jean, I am not so good with young baboons. I can see the difference in the large and middle-sized ones but the youngsters all tend to look the same to me.

There was a particular juvenile that formed an unusual attachment to me. Jean had already named her older brother Basil, after Basil Brush, a popular fox puppet on television at the time. We called his mother Foxy and so I named her juvenile daughter Vixen. Vixen one day surprised me by approaching as I sat outside on the back doorstep. To my utter amazement, she started picking at my head and hair, and then proceeded to groom me.

Baboons spend hours grooming each other and we have never seen a tick or any other form of parasite on them, unless they are very ill; they are meticulously clean when it comes to their own body hair. Vixen must have thought I was not so clean as, to my horror, every now and then she appeared to be eating something she had discovered in my hair. I think, or at least I hope, it was just a familiar mannerism, but she certainly made Jean and the staff laugh. On my side, I felt immensely honoured that a wild baboon showed such trust in me and clearly liked spending time grooming me.

The grooming became a regular occurrence and Vixen grew up being photographed, which she loved. She became accustomed to 'posing' for the paparazzi, be it me, visitors or volunteers. Whenever I gave a presentation overseas about our work, photos of Vixen were part of the show. Everyone was amazed that this wild-born baboon had taken to grooming a human. We knew that hand-reared baboons will do this to their adoptive mums, but to have a wild baboon, with her own family, include me as a member was an honour I treasured.

Among the males were several very special individuals to whom we formed attachments. Strangely, they were usually not the dominant males, and were often ranked quite low down in the baboon pecking order, as was Vixen's family too. There was Eric, Joe, Sassy, Yogi, and later Red, Zorro, Tiny, Petite and young Eric.

Older Eric was killed by the land invaders who were poaching in our area in the bad years. They hunted him with their dogs, chasing him up a tree and then attacking him with stones and rocks. Having killed him, they cut up his body in order to sell the meat, which they would pass off as another kind of meat. This often happens at the markets, the poachers lying to their customers as generally Zimbabweans don't knowingly eat baboon or monkey meat.

Eric's death broke our hearts. Jean had heard the dogs and knew something bad was going on and that it was close by. He had rushed off in that direction and found the poachers busy cutting up the carcass. The hunters ran off with their dogs and Jean recovered Eric's dismembered body. There was no doubt in our minds it was him. I buried his remains near the river.

Local Zimbabweans who have come here are always surprised at the relationship we have with these baboons. We have had to adapt, in that we do not want them to come into the house; they would break everything and, being baboons, defecate or pee almost anywhere! We cannot leave our external doors open and we even need to lock them, as some of the baboons have learnt how to open doors. They are so very clever. Our windows are gauze, not glass, allowing fresh air to flow through the house. Occasionally the baboons have broken the gauze mesh when chasing each other and bouncing against a window; and Vixen would pick at the gauze with her very long fingernails, making a minute hole, and then pick at the hole until it was large enough to pull open, and wide enough for her to enter the house. When this happened, Squiggle mongoose would have absolutely no fear in propelling herself at Vixen, jaws open, teeth bared like a manic shark. Unbelievably, Vixen, who probably weighed about 20 kilograms, would flee from this tiny monster! Then I had to be quick enough to open the door so Vixen could escape before she was bitten by a very mad Squiggle.

We have also learnt to be exceedingly careful about leaving anything lying around in the house that the baboons can see through the windows. No food or interesting-looking items, no medicines or decorations from the bush, such as a baobab pod or wooden banana pod, as this just encourages the baboons to attempt to break in and steal whatever they fancy. Cushions cannot be left outside on the chairs or they would head off into the blue yonder, carried off by very pleased-looking baboons. Washing can no longer be hung on the lines if the baboons are at home. They love stealing Jean's very nice European shirts and occasionally you can see a ghost running around in the bush, just a white shirt with furry legs. So I have become even tidier, as I want the baboons to stay.

I can walk in the bush with the house troop as if I am a member of their own family. Some of the baboons take food from our hands and can often be very gentle in their approach. We have learnt that if ever they are angry or afraid, for whatever reason, all we have to do is open our hands with our palms upwards to show we are not carrying any kind of weapon, like a stone or catapult, and then they completely calm down and relax.

Sassy was an amazing male who, like Vixen, took a shine to me and whenever I met him in the bush we would walk together for a long time as if I were just part of his extended family.

Living and working for wild animals and feeling as I do about them has led to some criticism. A couple of people with a more scientific approach have even gone as far as telling me that I anthropomorphise wild animals, attributing human thoughts and emotions to them. However, the longer I live with all these different animal species, the more I see them behaving in so many ways exactly as we do. Of course they have emotions, like gratitude, grief and pain and even, sometimes, they feel love for a human being.

Joe was more than a baboon, and I formed a special bond with him. He had such a gentle and lovely nature, particularly for a very large male baboon, probably the biggest male of them all. Joe looked like a huge teddy bear; he was pretty solidly built, with a soft, cuddly-looking jawline and a square face, unlike some of the others whose faces were narrower and not as cute. For years we considered him to be part of our family.

Unlike Yogi (see Rescued animals, chapter 6), Joe had always taken food from my hand. As one of the subservient members of the troop, he had to be careful not to get too close to food when the dominant members were around. Accompanied by his females, he would arrive at our house after the dominant members had left to forage for the day, and hang around for quite a few hours, enjoying the snacks. Then he stopped coming for a couple of weeks and when, one morning in 2015, he returned it was clear that something had happened during that time.

He arrived at the house looking very sick and I knew he had come to me for help. He was stiff in his hindquarters and when he walked he limped badly. With his hair matted and dry, he looked really ill. We have in our time had a baboon come in with rabies, but then the symptoms were obvious. That baboon displayed erratic behaviour, couldn't drink, his jaw was not working normally and he was extremely run down. He went away and never came back, so we assumed he had died. Joe, however, was not in any way exhibiting those kinds of symptoms. It was as if he had fallen out of a tree or been hit, maybe by a predator, but there were no cuts on his body;

he was just in a lot of pain. He needed help now, and we would have to look at human ways to help him, such as with antibiotics and anything else we had at our disposal. He also needed feeding up as he had lost so much weight.

I emailed a friend who is a vet and the kindest man I have ever had the pleasure of meeting. Kevin Lenahan is Irish and lives in the UK. He initially became a hippo supporter by adopting two hippos, one for himself and one for his partner, Natasha. In time I was fortunate to get to know him via email. Then, when I gave my first hippo presentations around the UK in 2005, I finally got to meet them both and a friendship was born. Whenever I had a sick animal, be it domestic or wild, I would email Kevin and he would come back to me with suggestions and tell me about various treatments that would be in the post to me the next day. He has always sent medicines and help for all our animals over the years and he has never wanted a dollar for his kindness. He is just the best.

For Joe we tried everything: all the medicines Kevin sent, special feeding of fruit and good quality food, but he was not improving. At times he seemed to be getting a bit stronger, but then he would deteriorate again. After a few months it was obvious that whatever was ailing him wasn't going to go away. Baboons have to climb trees, the higher the better, so that at night they are safe from predators. One morning I heard this pitiful calling and I found Joe up one of the taller mopane trees and he appeared stuck. His sore and aching body was not allowing him to climb down again and he was panicking.

I spent three hours talking to him and telling him to come down carefully, and eventually he did just that. It was awful seeing how slowly he had to move to climb down from that tree. There was no way he would be able to climb up again that night. So I devised a plan. I put some hay bales in the empty garage, arranged in a kind of boma shape so that there was an entrance but the bales sheltered the occupant from the wind, or from the eyes of a predator. I then coaxed Joe (as I once had Yogi, who had become ensnared in a poacher's wire trap) into the garage and, like Yogi, he limped his way behind me into his new home. He seemed to know instinctively that the bales were for him to lie within and so he propped himself up against them and drank some water that I had put there for him.

For the next month I fed him there and gave him water and vitamins and food, anything we could think of to make him healthier, but nothing was working. I gave him an old tree stump as I realised he might prefer something rather more natural than the bales of hay to prop himself up against, and he straightaway accepted the stump. Also, it was a lot less prickly. His huge brown eyes followed me as I worked around the garage. I even moved a chair into the garage and sat there with my laptop so I could talk to him and keep him company for some of the day.

I saw that he was desperate to interact with his own small family. They consisted of three females and their babies, which were probably his own children. So when the main troop had moved off, I left the gate open. Joe's family always stayed nearby and soon they were joining him in the garage. The babies would crawl around him or on him, and instead of this annoying him he really seemed to like having their company. Joe was such a kind and special baboon.

During this time I was talking to baboon experts around Africa, using Facebook for contacts. There was so much advice but, sadly, nothing helped. Then Joe started getting bedsores as he could no longer move around. This huge male baboon, weighing in at probably around 30 kilograms, allowed Jean and me to turn him over regularly so that the sores did not get worse. But it was clear that he was not getting better.

The nearest vet with the requisite knowledge about wildlife lives a seven-hour drive away, and there was no-one closer who could advise me. I knew Joe was getting worse. I contacted Rosemary, but she was away. However, Jess had just recently got her own darting license. I told her the problem and said I thought that perhaps we were not being kind to Joe and it would be better to let him go. But there was absolutely no way that Jean or I could shoot him – he was too much part of our lives. I asked Jess if she had some kind of drug that could do the deed, and she did. She was not too happy about it, but she understood the need and so agreed that the following day she would come down to us.

I talked to Joe and explained what I was going to do and said that I knew he wasn't getting better and that he was in a lot of pain. I asked his acceptance and forgiveness. Jess arrived the following morning with another colleague and her first words to me were 'Karen, are you okay?' Well, that did me in. I burst into tears and couldn't stop crying.

Jessica, like Rosemary, is an accomplished scientist and has spent many years dealing with snared wild dogs and all of the many woes Africa can throw at its wildlife. She also cares a lot about people; she could see that I was getting very worked up, and she was more worried about me than Joe. Jess was also scared that the drug she needed to give him wouldn't have the desired effect quickly enough. We discussed the situation, but I could see that she wasn't fully relaxed about what she had to do.

Eventually we went out to look at Joe and she said, 'You know, he doesn't want to go. He is still wanting to fight. It's in his eyes.' And that was it! I said, 'I can't do this. I am so sorry to bring you all this way and now say this, but let's not do it.'

Jessica has the most beautiful and greenest of eyes and they were full of compassion as she looked at me. 'Karen, I really do understand. No problem. Take care of you and him and call me if you change your mind later'. With that she packed up her stuff and she and her colleague drove off.

I went back to Joe and talked and talked to him, telling him that all I wanted for him was the best and for him somehow to be a healthy baboon again, living with his family out in the bush. But he looked at me with those huge eyes and I knew and he knew that it couldn't be. For two days he hung on, but his body was progressively shutting down.

Jean-Roger was away and was due back the next day. When he came home he looked at Joe and said, 'Karen, it really is time. He is hanging on for you, but not for himself. He needs to go'.

So once again I contacted Jess and asked if she could come back the next day. She agreed, and told me she had done a lot of research on what dosage to give him and that she felt more confident now.

That night I gave Joe special treats and sat with him until very late, stroking his fur and softly singing to him. I went to bed exhausted – more emotionally than physically. I had been trying to save his life for over four months and now I had to admit defeat. At five the following morning Jean went outside to organise the rangers and he took a walk to the garage. He woke me by gently touching my face. 'Karen, Joe has gone.'

These were the words I heard as I opened my eyes.

My darling Joe baboon had left us in the early hours of the morning. At first I was devastated that I had not been there with him, but as Jean said to me, 'Joe left quietly, on his own, for you, Karen, so that you wouldn't have to bring Jess to put him to sleep. He gave you one last parting gift'.

I was crying hysterically. I dragged on my clothes and ran outside and down to the garage, and sat beside my boy. He looked so peaceful, so soft; even his fur looked better. My Joe had chosen to go and had passed to the other world. Jean contacted Jess and told her the news.

We buried Joe outside our bedroom alongside all our departed domestic animals from over the years. I put his leaning tree stump on the grave. I contacted a very kind South African Facebook friend, Lynette Johnson, who also has a profound rapport with baboons. She has worked with baboon sanctuaries for many years and she asked me to put a pretty rock on Joe's grave. I had a gorgeous white quartz crystal, so that, too, is now upon the grave.

The pain of loss takes so long to pass, and grief for those that we love never really goes away. When quite a bit of time had passed I could finally remember Joe with lightness, and the joy he gave to me.

9

Adventures in the bush

Over the years quite a number of people have come to stay at the Turgwe Hippo Trust as paying volunteers. Many charities, supporting both animals and humans, offer such an experience. Some people are surprised when I tell them that there is a fee to volunteer or stay as a tourist. They think that by offering their experience or desire to help that this should be enough. What they don't appreciate is that to operate any kind of charity or not-for-profit organisation there are all the daily running costs and staff to pay, and that in order to keep a charity organisation going one is absolutely dependent on the kindness of others.

During the northern hemisphere summer, people are holidaying and spending time with their families, and fundraising always slows down for us during those months. Volunteers, however, make up the huge deficit in fundraising during this period – our wintertime. The volunteers pay to stay during these months and their donations, once the costs of their stay are removed, help to run the Trust.

I decided to take on volunteers in 1999, with my first volunteer going on to run her own project for helping elephants in Zimbabwe. It was rewarding to think that perhaps having volunteered with us and others like us had helped her to change her own life, and inspired her to do what she did so very well for 'her elephants'. Over time other volunteers have gone on to start projects that had hitherto been a distant dream for them, and they tell me that their stay at Hippo Haven gave them that added push to succeed and follow their dream. So not only do the volunteers really help the Turgwe Hippo Trust to keep going financially, but we like to think that, in however small a way, we help these people to reach for the stars and find what they want in life. All our volunteers, without exception, have loved the intimacy of our home and the fact that we live with wild animals rather than that they live with us. One never quite knows what you may find at the front or back door and sometimes it can cause quite a bit of apprehension.

Snakes do not sit well with most people but in winter, when the volunteers are normally around, the snakes are all sleeping as it's far too cold for them to be about. (I, too, stay in my bed longer than normal as it's extremely cold in the early mornings and at night.) Occasionally a snake may come out from its resting place to bask in the winter sun, but it's highly unlikely for them to be as prevalent in winter as they are during the summer rains. Another reason why we prefer to have our visitors in the dry season is that there are generally far fewer spiders and insects around, including mosquitos, so there is also far less chance of catching malaria than there is during our hot, wet months.

Many friends come to visit from overseas. One friend, Jenny Bowen, first came here from the UK with an organisation then called Operation Raleigh. Jenny was one of Operation Raleigh's team leaders, bringing a group of 17- and 18-year-olds on the adventure of their lives. The programme offered training and support in the fields of community, adventure and conservation, and the Conservancy took on volunteers over a period of five years. During this time Jenny and I formed a lasting friendship.

She has gone on to be an extremely successful tour leader, author and entrepreneur, running her own company, Sense Earth, and taking all kinds of people and students around parts of southern Africa to participate in projects for people and animals alike. In those early years she was learning about what she would do – and excel at – later, so the animals and snakes of Africa were all new for this very bright English girl.

Once when Jenny came to stay with me while Jean-Roger was away working, she and I spent as much time as possible in the bush, enjoying quality time together. Jenny had arrived just as our home reached near-completion, with only the bathroom to finish. She had a bed inside, while I continued to sleep outside under our canvas awning. We were still using our outside long-drop toilet: a lean-to building with no door, where you sat perched above the deep pit, on a bricked-up base with a proper toilet seat, watching the birds and monkeys feeding in the trees. A loo with a view.

It was dark and Jenny wanted to visit the toilet. Carrying a torch, she went to open the front door. The door frame is made of local pod mahogany hardwood from the bush, with gauze mesh attached to the frame in place of glass. The light from her torch caught movement and I heard a shriek.

'Karen, there is a snake on the front step and it's moving!'

I came over to investigate and, sure enough, a Mozambique spitting cobra, probably just under two metres long, was investigating the porch and in no hurry to leave.

'Not a problem, just go out the back door', I said casually.

Soon there was another shriek, and this time it was delivered with even more anguish and urgency as Jenny's need to pee was growing with every second.

'There's another one out here! I'm not sure if it's dead or not, and it's lying directly on the step! Karen, I really need to pee!'

I was bemused as there on the back step was the second snake, not even the same species, but a fat, healthy puff adder, at least one metre long, curled up asleep but definitely very much alive.

'Oh, we have a bit of an issue now, as both snakes can hurt you rather badly and I don't think opening the door is a good plan right at this moment as that will just annoy them.'

She was by now biting her lip. 'Karen, that's it! Two snakes in one night when my bladder is fit to burst. Can I go and pee in the bath?' Well, what can a friend say? When we looked much later both snakes had moved on, unaware of the drama they had caused, but I don't think Jenny and I ever forgot that experience.

Another snake incident happened with the Trust's very first volunteer, Sharon Picot, who went on to work for nine years with the elephants in Hwange, known in Zimbabwe as the President's herd. Sharon was a high-flying executive who regularly volunteered in Africa and had finally found her niche in Hwange, where she ended up running, single-handedly, her own project for the elephants. When she stayed with me she had already volunteered in other African countries, but it was her first time of volunteering with a hippo charity. We had some weird, sad and wonderful experiences, some of which are mentioned in my first book, but the snake incident happened right at the very beginning – although not before an incident with our monkeys.

I'd picked up Sharon from a safari camp some 50 kilometres away, and noted that she was wearing a black T-shirt with a picture of a lion on the front. We drove home talking all the time, getting to know each other. She was Australian, gutsy and full of spirit. As we arrived at the house the monkeys were there to greet us, all 35 of them. As Sharon got out of the car a very strange thing happened. All the monkeys, without exception, became extremely aggressive, staring at her as if she were from outer space, chattering and giving angry alarm calls. Even though monkeys are tiny compared with baboons, when 35 of them are that angry they take on a different shape, and with their eyes tight and eyebrows being raised up and down in alarm, they looked very ferocious. A few of the males began posturing as if they were about to attack her. I was completely puzzled as the monkeys are normally so gentle and had never before behaved like that with anyone. I looked at her startled face and then it clicked: the monkeys were not acting like this because of her, but it was the very realistic painting of the lion on her T-shirt that was disturbing them. Lions are natural predators and in the monkeys' eyes Sharon was a lion. She covered the pic by holding her bag in front of it as I quickly led her to her cottage, suggesting she change tops. I was sure this would calm the monkeys.

She did as I suggested and sure enough, as she came out of the door with a plain shirt on, not one monkey batted an eyelid. They all resumed their normal behaviour as if nothing at all had occurred. It was quite extraordinary to see such a turnaround and it taught me yet another lesson about monkeys, and about advice to give visitors coming to the bush.

Not five minutes had passed when I heard a loud exclamation. Sharon shouted, 'Karen, I don't fucking believe it, there is a snake here on the corner of the thatch and it's checking me out in a very unfriendly way.'

I shot around the house to find out what was trying to kill the Trust's first volunteer and there was the culprit.

Our baboons, like all baboons, can be very destructive, and so we had tried everything we could think of to keep them from wrecking the thatch on our house. They love to pull out handfuls of thatch, and when you live with more than 55 baboons they can very quickly turn a nicely thatched, rainproof roof into something that definitely won't be waterproof once the rains start.

My latest idea had been to purchase four rubber snakes and put one on each corner of the house, hoping that the baboons' natural aversion to reptiles would keep them from climbing up the corners on to the roof. I had forgotten that the snakes were there as they had only been up for a few days, and the snake that Sharon was so afraid of and which was giving her the evil eye was a lovely black rubber chap! I must say, he was very realistic looking, so it wasn't as if she had been fooled by a poor imitation. She shrieked and swore even louder when I moved forward and picked the snake up; and then she saw the funny side of it and we had a good laugh.

Sharon's two weeks with us were full of laughter, and I was immensely proud of her when she achieved her goal of working with elephants. She wrote some memorable books about her nine years of living with those amazing animals. I also got to visit her on a few occasions and we would have wonderful experiences, such as when wild elephants stood right by her vehicle as she scratched the tusks of a couple of them, or when over 200 individuals all walked past in single file, within touching distance of the car, with baby ellies frolicking alongside them. And I admit that every time she took me into the bush and we witnessed such extraordinary interactions, I would cry – tears of total love, astonishment and wonder, as well as tears of sadness that humans could ever hurt such majestic and peace-loving animals. I shed tears for all of the wild animals. I wished ardently that those who hunt and kill elephants for sport, money or food could sit here with us and feel the incredible joy that one can share with wild animals if you have trust in them and wish them no harm. Sharon had learnt what she could and couldn't do, and the results were just mind blowing.

While accompanied by volunteers in the bush, I have had the odd encounter with animals where I have had to manage a potentially dangerous situation. Having been a safari guide, I have a bit of an edge on how to behave with wild animals. Of course, not only do all the volunteers sign an indemnity form to cover the Trust, but I explain to them how they must behave when we walk in the bush, and that they must listen to me at all times as it can be a matter of life and death if they don't. If you approach a so-called dangerous wild animal in the wrong way, you mustn't feel outraged if the animal defends itself against this intrusion into its space.

My rule is 'do not disturb animals'. As an onlooker, you may be lucky enough, with time, to connect with wildlife as I have been able to do with the hippos, and as Sharon did with the elephants, and Kim, another friend, with hyenas. We are not in the safari business, we are not in any kind of business, we are running an animal charity and the animals come first in every way; so I always remain unobtrusive and don't in any way attempt to alter the animals' natural behaviour.

To do this I use my senses – sight, sound and smell – and I don't ever carry a weapon. I hold the thought that it's far safer to be unarmed than to have false confidence about being able to protect myself and the people with me. People must be aware of the possible dangers and they must also understand that they have agreed to be here in our home and hence must follow the wildlife rules.

It doesn't mean there will never be an incident, but I am prepared to risk my own life rather than that of anyone who is under my care – no volunteer or visitor should be hurt. By the same token, the bush is not always predictable and animals, like us, can have 'bad-hair days' when they may do something quite abnormal and, if you are not alert, could prove to be dangerous.

The rangers for the Trust are not armed for various reasons. One is that you can just as easily avoid being harmed by using common sense and your own physical abilities; often a rifle would be more of a hindrance than a help in an emergency situation. I know of several buffalo attacks where the person was armed and still got hurt. Another reason is that rangers with rifles have been known to shoot at animals that they claimed were attacking them, when in fact the rangers were poaching. This has not happened to us, but it has to other people that we know. As we are not in the business of taking clients on safari, we are not obliged to carry weapons and all visitors to us come here at their own risk.

Buffalos can be very dangerous, but usually only if they are injured. Unlike most injured animals, who just want to hide away as they try to recover, a buffalo reacts with anger, and anyone who crosses their path is fair game. If a buffalo is carrying a wound or snare, or has been shot by hunters and somehow managed to escape the situation, he may retaliate against any available human. They are even known to stalk and deliberately hunt humans when they are injured. And once a buffalo has killed a person it becomes a very dangerous animal. The African name for such an animal is 'black death', which says it all.

Herbert, a ranger who used to work for the Trust, had a very near miss with a wounded buffalo. We had received information that a poacher who was operating in another area about eight kilometres from our home had been found gored to death by a buffalo. We told the rangers to be on high alert when in the bush and, if they caught sight of a lone buffalo, to head straight for the nearest rocky koppie or large tree, just in case it was the wounded bull.

Jean-Roger had to go off to South Africa to buy goods for the Trust, so I was left to cope with my own work as well as his, which includes telling the rangers where to patrol morning and afternoon, and occasionally following up on them to check they are going where we have sent them. I was working at my desk when I heard my name called and found Elijah, one of the rangers, sweating and clearly in a bad state. He informed me that Herbert was dead. Or at least that is what I thought he said; he was only semi-coherent as he must have run quite some distance.

Once I had managed to get him to calm down, the story unfolded. He said they were on their patrol when suddenly, about 10 metres in front of them, a buffalo exploded from a thicket on to the track and the two men ran for their lives. Elijah did not stop until he reached a large mopane tree and, after climbing it, he could hear Herbert screaming but he couldn't see him. He assumed the buffalo had killed Herbert and, when all was quiet again, Elijah had been too afraid to go forward and find out, so instead he returned, at a run, to alert me.

It had happened about four kilometres from the house, but it would have been completely crazy for me to go there alone, and Elijah was in no state to accompany me. I ran to switch on the generator and, once the satellite dish had begun tracking, I had wi-fi and could contact someone. I got hold of one of the managers on the neighbouring property, Humani, and asked if they could contact the police support unit and Roger Whittall's rangers. I told them what had happened and said that the quicker they got to me, the better, just in case Herbert was still alive.

Like Elijah, I didn't hold out too much hope. From the level of aggression it had shown, this had to be the same buffalo that had earlier killed the poacher, and this did not bode well for Herbert. Given the seriousness of the situation, I also wanted Jean to know what was happening and managed to send a message to him.

While I was fearing the worst and feeling pretty panicky, to my utter astonishment I saw Herbert walking, or should I say staggering, into camp. He had blood dripping from a head wound, also running down his right arm, and he was limping quite badly, but he was alive. I don't normally hug our staff, but I couldn't help myself this time. I threw my arms around Herbert and held him for a second, although I could see that he was in complete shock. I made him sit down and lean against one of the trees as he really was unsteady on his feet, then I rushed to get disinfectant and bandages and cloths and warm water. It amazed me how he had managed to walk all that way home. In cleaning the wounds I was very happy to find that none were too deep or too serious and no bones were broken.

I gave him sweet tea and two painkillers and as he became more coherent, he told me what had happened. The buffalo had chased after him as he had been closest to the bush it had come out of, so Herbert, remembering what I had told them, ran straight for a nearby koppie. As he ran up the rocks he realised the buffalo was following and was going to catch up with him. He noticed a large boulder on one side of the track he was running along, so he threw himself down on the ground and crawled to the boulder, wedging himself into a rather small crack. He still had his wooden stick, carried by all the rangers to use as protection against attack by humans or animals.

The rock shielded most of Herbert's body but the buffalo knew he was tucked in there, so the crazed animal proceeded to try and dig him out; but because of the awkward angle, it didn't dig in the usual way, using its mighty boss and horns, but rather pawed at Herbert with a front foot. A hoof connected with Herbert's head and then his arm, and that's how both were injured. Herbert used his stick to beat at the buffalo's leg and this had the desired effect as the beast backed off. He did not go far and, as he milled around near the rock, Herbert quite clearly saw that the buffalo had a very long and thick snare embedded in his right back leg. It had cut right into the bone; he must have been carrying it for a long time. No wonder he was so angry and aggressive – he was in considerable pain.

Herbert couldn't move or try to get home while the buffalo was still there; all he could do was lie there bleeding and in pain, but alive. It was only when he saw that the buffalo had gone that he found the courage to leave the rock and begin his walk home and, fortunately for Herbert, he did not have another encounter with his attacker. He had just finished telling me what had happened when in drove the support unit of Roger's two rangers and one National Parks scout. All three of them were armed.

They spoke briefly to Herbert and then told me they would go and find the buffalo, but they needed Elijah with them to show them the exact area. They said they were going to shoot it as it had already killed a man. Bringing in a person who could dart the animal and remove the snare was not going to happen. This buffalo had to die. I couldn't argue with them as, in the end, National Parks have full authority in such a situation. And I knew there was nobody close enough to come and dart the animal as both Rosemary and Jess were away. From what Herbert had said it sounded as if the wound was too far gone anyway.

Four hours later they returned with the dead buffalo loaded in the back of the Land Cruiser. I went over to see it and Herbert was not wrong, the snare had practically severed most of the nerves in the buffalo's leg near the foot, and it must have been in agony. It was a buffalo in its prime, neither young nor old, but it had already lost condition as the pain must have made it difficult to move around and graze freely, or to cover large enough areas to find food.

Herbert did not want me to drive him all the way to Chiredzi to the local hospital. It has an awful reputation and once before he had been there with very bad malaria and he told us afterwards he would rather be dead than go back to that hospital. So, as I was sure there was nothing internally damaged or broken, I agreed. Herbert had been exceedingly lucky. He spent four days resting at the rangers' house in our camp. Jean finally got the message about the dramatic events and when he came home we certainly had a lot to talk about!

10

Success stories

I have always believed that we should leave wild animals to heal in their own time, in their natural habitat. However, over the years many animals and birds have come into our lives which, without our intervention, would simply never have survived. As with Joe baboon and some of the warthogs, there have been times when, out of compassion, we have stepped in to help them. We have found animals and birds in the bush that have lost their parents, which was probably what had happened to Squiggle mongoose (see chapter 7). Without my bringing her home and looking after her she would have died. To save the life of a wild animal and see it return to its natural environment brings about mixed emotions, depending on how long the animal has been living with you; and pure joy if you have the privilege of seeing it again, once it has been freed and has successfully reintegrated into the wild.

We have found birds particularly rewarding in this way, as often, when released, they either remain in the vicinity of our home for a while or at least pay us visits. To watch a bird flying free again, that wouldn't have made it without one's assistance, is deeply rewarding. There have been many such birds, but two, in particular, stand out in my mind.

Often nightjars and coursers will sit on roads at night, waiting to catch insects and absorbing the heat from the sand, tar or dirt track during the colder months. One evening just after dusk Jean-Roger drove into camp, and to my dismay I saw a dead bird attached to his front bumper. Even before he had left the vehicle I was at the bumper trying to identify the bird and detach it. It was then that I noticed it move. It was attached to the bumper by one of its legs and part of the wing, and both looked either badly dislocated or broken. It was an adult Three-banded courser.

Holding the bird gently, I carefully unwrapped its leg from the bumper. By then Jean had joined me and was very surprised and cross with himself as he hadn't seen the bird sitting on the road or noticed the light of its eyes in the headlights. And, as is their habit, it must have tried to lift off at the last minute, just as he drove over it, and hence got caught in the bumper. I told him not to stress, but to help me make a temporary home for the bird. There was no sign of an open wound and hopefully, as Jean had been driving very slowly on the dirt road, no internal injury. Because it was Valentine's Day, we didn't hesitate to name him Valentine.

As it so happened, Jean had nearly finished building an outside run for two of our rescue cats who live in one of the volunteers' cottages, and was designed so that the cats could go about their ablutions at night in safety. No-one was visiting us at the time as it was our rainy season, so Jean quickly shut off the opening from the cottage to the run, and I added some loose leaves, soil and dry grass to the cage, as well as a dish of water. I put Valentine into his (hopefully) temporary home. He could stand on one of his legs but the other was a bit out of shape, and one of his wings looked rather bent, but neither looked broken. I left him for the night so he could rest and perhaps recover, hoping that by morning he would be a lot better.

I have found that it's often shock that makes animals appear to be at death's door and, after a while, as long as they are in a warm and quiet place, they completely recover. In Valentine's case it was a bit more than shock as he was still one-legged in the morning, though the wing was settling and not sticking out as badly. I knew he had to eat and just hoped that he would do so, in spite of being captive. I got Silas to capture some grasshoppers and popped them into the cage and, to my joy, within seconds Valentine was eating them. The good thing was that I could push grasshoppers and batches of Squiggle's mealworms through the wire mesh and he would feed himself, which made him walk around inside the enclosure and exercise his legs. Because of the limited space he couldn't move too far, though, and would be able to heal while being fed.

Coursers look a lot like plovers, but have longer legs. Valentine had the diagnostic three bands of brown, black and chestnut across his throat and breast. Luckily, because coursers are mostly crepuscular and spend the main part of the day resting in the shade of a bush or tree, he was not excessively disturbed by his new confined living quarters. If coursers are afraid they will typically freeze and then set off at a run, only taking flight at the very last moment; and they normally don't fly over long distances.

For the next five weeks Valentine lived with us and slowly his damaged leg straightened. The enforced rest, limited movement and plenty of good food all helped to heal his injuries. He fed voraciously and, thanks to daily contact with humans, he became considerably tamer. But he was still a wild bird, and I intended to release him as soon as I felt that he could survive.

The day came when I was sure Valentine was fully healed and capable of going back to his normal life. I didn't want to release him in the area where Jean had likely hit him as that road is used by the people who invaded the area back in the early 2000s. There are also a few huts nearby and I was worried that the dogs might sniff him out, and if he was still a bit weak he would be vulnerable. So instead Jean and I took him to a semi-open area where the hippos often graze at night, about two kilometres away from the accident scene. We carried Valentine in one of our larger cat containers. With any release I feel pretty choked-up, my heart batters away and I am always scared that I am either releasing too early or that something could go wrong. I have to be very strict with myself and think, 'you are setting it free as it no longer needs you and it has to return to the life it was born to lead'. I have to have faith that the universe will deliver, and the animal will be okay and continue its former wild existence.

We put the container down and I opened it, and nothing happened: Valentine remained inside. So gently, very carefully, I lifted him out and took him over to a nearby thick bush. I placed him there and told him I loved him and backed off, hoping he would either run or fly off. For minutes he played out the usual courser freezing stance and then shook himself as if waking up from a dream and slowly started walking around. Then he gave what appeared to be a little leap of joy and took off for a few metres in flight before landing again and running very fast to another thick bush. He was back to being a wild bird. As always, my tears flowed as I watched him doing what he was meant to do, and then we drove home.

The greatest honour that a released animal can bestow upon you is to recognise you later, and approach or visit you. Valentine turned out to do exactly that. I went back to the release site the following day, but there was no sign of him. I told myself he had found a place that he was happy to rest up in and that I had to be satisfied with this ending. I went back at least five times, but there was no sign of him at all, so I had to move on in my thoughts and emotions.

Then, about one week after his release, I was at home at dusk and I heard the familiar call of a courser. I stepped outside and was instantly intrigued as there in the back yard, strutting around on the bare earth, was a Three-banded courser. I called Jean-Roger and he joined me.

'Could it be Valentine? Has he found our home, and if so, is he okay?' I mused.

Jean looked at him. 'Well, you know what to do – approach him and see what happens. Offer him a couple of mealworms and if he takes them that will be proof that it's him.'

Sure enough, as I got closer to the bird, instead of running off or taking flight he just looked at me, so I threw a couple of worms in his direction – and lo and behold, he ate them. It was Valentine. He hung around for about 30 minutes and then took flight and was gone and he never came home again.

I like to think that Valentine was showing me how he was getting on, and that I need no longer be afraid for him. It was yet another connection with wildlife, and it left me filled with the most incredible feeling of peace and happiness.

Then there was Lizzie. We found her during a drought, an event that is sadly quite common in our low-rainfall area. And an extended drought can be disastrous for the vegetation and, consequently, the animals it supports. At such times I step in and feed the hippos and any other wildlife, knowing that otherwise the animals would die.

Early one afternoon, Jean and I had taken a walk before it would be time for me to go off with the rangers in the vehicle and start laying out food for all the animals. This is an intensive operation and very hard work, and something I have done only five times in three decades. I feed hay as a bulk feed and then add horse cubes and survival ration – a mixture of the failed crops and molasses, which we add to attract the grazers. At that time I was feeding 24 hippos and over 250 other wild animals. Even the elephants were now coming in to feed. On average, the two rangers and I laid out about two tons of food daily in 18 different feeding stations in the bush. It's thanks to the Turgwe Hippo Trust's generous supporters that we have been able to roll out these rescue programmes.

It was a very hot day, a little over 40 degrees centigrade, and as we came down one of the dry riverbed tracks I spotted something lying still. It was a small raptor fledgling, a bird that has just learnt to fly, but this little bird was in a bad way. Her bill was open as she gasped for air and she was completely dehydrated; it looked as though she would expire at any minute. I took the cap off our water bottle and held it under her bill and she enthusiastically started sipping the water, which was most unusual and showed how desperately dehydrated she was.

I picked her up – there was no way we could leave her in the heat on the road and expect her to survive. It is not easy to carry a raptor, even a small to medium-sized bird or fledgling, as they have exceeding sharp claws with which she was hanging on to my arm and hand, but I had to get her home. It was so hot that, as we walked, we kept coming across birds sitting in trees with their bills open. The road was even hotter, with no breeze, nothing at all, and not a drop of water in sight.

At the house we took Squiggle's small travelling cage, originally a hamster cage, and pushed a couple of branches through the wire sides on which the bird could perch. I added a dish of water that was not too deep, but deep enough for her to get in and wash her feathers if she so desired. Then we hung the cage from a rafter where no Squiggle or any of our rescue cats could get at it and left her to rest.

Later I went back to her and she was sitting on a branch looking far happier. She had been in the water and had more to drink, as shown by the appearance of her eyes, which were now much clearer and looked more alive; she had even got her feathers wet. I offered her a tiny bit of raw chicken, which she took straightaway. I think she must have been sitting on that track for some time and, had we not come along when we did, she would probably soon have died.

Lizzie, as I named her, was one of Zimbabwe's small raptors, a Lizard buzzard, with a recognisable black stripe on the underside of the neck and down the breast. These raptors eat lizards and small birds, so she liked raw chicken, which was the best we could give her and, of course, the occasional dead chicks when we could get them from Chiredzi. I hated collecting the chicks, which are fed until they reach a certain size before being sent to town, where they are sold live for their meat. The unfortunate chicks arrive at the depot in town, crammed into cardboard boxes. Lots die while being transported in such a horrid manner, often spending several hours on top of a bus or in somebody's hot vehicle. Lizzie, however, would happily pluck at the chicks and eat parts of the flesh that she enjoyed. Squiggle only ever ate the head.

Although thoroughly revived by now, Lizzie could still not be returned to where we had found her as there was no obvious sign of a nest or her parents, and she was too young to be able to fend for herself. The ongoing extreme heat was an added deterrent. She was growing rapidly on her diet of chicks and raw chicken, so we brought down Squiggle's larger cage, used on longer trips to Harare, and made it comfortable for Lizzie, with branches for her to sit on.

I knew she had to have fresh air and sunlight, so I moved her cage into our vegetable garden, which is protected from our home troop of baboons by a huge wired cage. I would take a chair and my laptop and sit working in the vegetable garden, talking to her and getting her used to being outside. Once she was old enough to sit on a perch, we put more branches into her cage and she would sit on these for hours. She was very curious about her surroundings and would walk up and down the perch checking out the scenery. Sometimes the baboons or the vervets would jump on to the roof of the cage to check out what we were doing, but in general they had better things to do than sit around with Lizzie and me. We always brought her back into the house at dusk as predators could easily hurt or stress her if she were left outside all night.

After a couple more weeks it was time to see if she could try flying again. She had put on weight and looked more like an adult now than a fluffy fledgling. I hoped she would be ready to try a few small flights. The vegetable garden enclosure was large enough for this purpose, and as it was completely fenced she would be safe. I began by holding a branch for her to perch on, then I would move with her towards another branch and gently give her bottom a little push. At first she jumped from me to the perch, but soon she started flapping her wings, and then one afternoon she took flight. Admittedly, the distance was short and within three flaps she had arrived on the perch, but it was a beginning. She was visibly proud of herself and puffed up her breast feathers as if to say, 'Hey, look at me, I can fly!' Within a few days she could fly from one end of the vegetable garden to the other without my aid. I was just like a very proud mum watching her child's first steps. I would talk to her constantly and praise her abilities while taking multiple pictures of our photogenic bird. Each day I made a small video showing her progress and I knew that it wouldn't be too long now before her release date was due.

My biggest concern about releasing her was whether she would know instinctively how to hunt or whether I should continue feeding her for a while. And, if released at our home, would she hang around us and allow me to provide her with food until she was able to catch her own prey?

It is stressful saving an animal or bird, but it's even more stressful when you take that final leap of faith and free them back into their natural habitat. I cannot bear to see any living thing kept in captivity against its will. Lizzie had to be given the chance to live as a Lizard buzzard should.

D-day arrived and Jean was tasked with taking a video of the event. I put Lizzie on to a loose branch, Jean opened the gate of the caged garden and I stepped outside. Lizzie took off within seconds, launching herself into her first flight outside of the cage. She circled the staff houses and then turned and landed in a tree near to where we were filming her flight, and then she just looked at us as if to say, 'Hey I did it! I knew I could, I just had to convince you.'

I spent the next hour watching her, and once more she took flight before returning to another tree close by. I asked Jean to bring me a lump of raw chicken as I had purposely not fed her that morning, keen to see if she would come back to me for food. I held it up for her to see. Raptors' eyesight is excellent, so I did not even have to wave the morsel around: she immediately saw what I had in my hand. I threw it a short distance away and waited. Happiness hit me with force as that clever little bird took flight and landed on the ground, grabbing the chicken in one foot and taking off to a tree branch, where she proceeded to pull off strips of meat and devour them.

This was just the best, for she had proved to me I could still feed her until she was able to hunt for herself. Now it would be a question of whether she would stay in our area or not. Later that afternoon she was still in the same tree, and by dusk that day she had moved to another larger tree nearby. For the following few days she stayed in our vicinity and I fed her twice a day, and then one day she was gone. Of course, doubt entered my mind and I worried that a larger raptor had attacked her or something else terrible had occurred. I had to stop thinking that way as it was not healthy, but for a worrier it's not easy to let go of fear and doubt.

Two days later Jean and I were walking in the area where we had found Lizzie when suddenly a bird swooped near us and landed in a tree. It was Lizzie. If it had been any other Lizard buzzard it wouldn't have allowed us to approach the tree as closely as we did without its taking flight: it was our Lizzie. I talked to her and told her how amazingly clever she was. She looked fine. Her crop was full, so she had fed herself, on what I would never know, but Lizzie could now hunt, which was just perfect. We stayed with her for a while and when we left I mentioned to Jean how interesting it was that she had returned to where we had found her originally. It is at least two kilometres from our home, but she had returned there, her natural instincts taking her back to where she was born.

We continued to see her for a couple of years, always in that area, and then one day she was gone. I like to think she found a mate and had her own chick and that she is still flying free. I am sure she is.

One day a huge male warthog, whom we named Arthur, walked into our back yard. He was full of warthog bravado, mock-charging any human or animal he saw and appearing very cheeky and full of himself. We could tell he was not young as his tusks were worn down, but still sharp enough to do some serious injury to our soft human flesh. He would come sniffing around, cropping our lawn, digging it up and making a lot of mess. I realised he was probably hungry, so I decided to put out some horse cubes and within minutes he was munching away. He normally arrived at the house in the late afternoon; then, to our surprise, he began hanging around the back door at dusk and often even later, sometimes up until nine or so at night. He must have felt safe with us, we supposed. But I worried because predators love warthogs and he should have been down one of the holes that they use at night, usually an old aardvark (antbear) burrow or one they have dug out for themselves.

For the next three years Arthur was a regular visitor. From the wild fellow who had arrived at our back door, he was now so 'tame' that he loved having his tummy scratched. If you started to scratch him he would collapse on the ground and then turn on his side so that you could give his tummy a good rubbing and scratching. Considering he was born wild and not hand raised, this was amazing.

One day he came in with a massive abscess on his neck. It was very swollen and must have been causing him a tremendous amount of pain as the pus was not able to escape, leading to all kinds of bad side effects. Jean was confident that he could cut the abscess with one of his model plane scalpels. The objective was to burst the skin so that the pus could ooze out, alleviating the pressure and pain.

Sure enough, Jean was not only right that Arthur would let him do this, but at one point Jean had to really hack at the abscess as Arthur's skin was very thick and tough. He felt that by 'working at it' enough, it would burst naturally once Arthur was moving around. For the entire time that Jean was busy, Arthur just lay on his side, allowing a human being to hack at his neck. This large wild warthog had allowed us to help him. When he arrived the following afternoon we could see that the abscess had burst. All the gunge and poison had been seeping out and already the swelling had reduced tremendously. All I can say is that his jaunty step was one of happiness; he was no longer in pain.

As the rainy season approached, Arthur made us even happier one afternoon when he came into the yard accompanied by a young female. She was in the beginning very nervous but, like Arthur, once she realised we were not going to hurt her she settled down with us. Two months later she arrived at the house with two little piglets, so Arthur our boy had become a dad and we were oh so proud!

Arthur and his family were the first of many warthogs that over the years made Hippo Haven homestead part of their territory. Nowadays we have over 40 in our area that we have fed, and 36 regular daily visitors. The wonderful thing is that we are able to continue feeding all of them a supplementary diet thanks to the Turgwe Hippo Trust supporters, who either adopt a hippo or donate to the Trust. We feed the animals to keep them safe from the people who want to kill them and who had killed so many warthogs when they first arrived. Thanks to the feeding, these animals tend to live in sounders close by, so we can keep a daily watch over them.

We suspect that my darling Arthur was finally one of the casualties to these poachers. In his memory I swore an oath that the Trust would look after any animal that came into our back yard and this has been the case ever since. Right now the baboons, vervet monkeys, warthogs and, of course, Steve hippo know that our home is a safe and welcoming haven.

11

Birth of a hippo

Sometimes when I am studying hippo behaviour I am witness to really astonishing events, and am left wondering if they are standard behaviour or are as extraordinary as they seem. It was April 2011 and I had just arrived at the pool that's closest to the house when I noticed a newborn calf lying next to Tacha in a very shallow part of the Turgwe River. As I watched, the calf took a deep breath of air and, with all its splashing around in the wet, some water must have got into its nostrils. Its tiny nose twitched in surprise at its first taste of home. Beside the calf, lying on her side, was Tacha; she knew her calf had to learn all by itself how to find her milk. And the hippo calf's only interest was in getting to that sweet-smelling milk, which was tantalisingly nearby – but where exactly? Relatively minute compared to its mother's one-and-a-half-ton bulk, the 20-kilogram calf was nevertess having difficulty balancing as it tried to stand up in the shallow channel of the riverbed and walk. Finally it succeeded and began its wobbling, staggering gait around its mother, searching for the nourishing food.

Tacha, from her reclining position, could see her calf taking baby steps alongside her body, a distance of nearly three metres – a long way to go for a newborn calf. She rolled further on to her side so that the calf would notice her udder tucked between her back legs, just like the udder of a cow. Her udder was not so obvious, though; it was covered by Tacha's massive belly and so the calf missed it the first time around and continued circling its mother.

Unbeknown to Tacha, two hungry crocodiles were watching from a few metres away, having witnessed the birth. As is the crocodile way, they relaxed in the water, waiting patiently for any advantage that would get them what they hoped for. Once more, the calf slipped and, exhausted, lay down to rest in the shallow water behind her mother's ample bottom. I could see that she was a little female.

One of the crocodiles moved with stealth, inching its way towards the calf. He was not a particularly large crocodile, rather a juvenile of around one-and-a-half metres, but very much larger than the baby hippo. I could see almost his entire body above the water, but as he drew closer to the calf he submerged. Nothing could be seen by mother or calf from above the water's surface as the crocodile swam directly towards the newborn baby.

As I looked on, my fear for the calf reached fever pitch. I knew there was absolutely nothing I could do to intervene. I was standing above the hippos, at the top of the steep riverbank from where I had been filming the calf as she took her first faltering steps around her mother. The slight movement caused by the crocodile heading in their direction had attracted my attention, and I stood frozen, watching as the crocodile submerged and closed in on the hippos. I was certain it would attack the newborn calf.

Minutes raced by, but nothing happened. The calf was again on her feet and this time she was heading in the right direction, straight towards the full udder. Her nose located the milk and at that moment Tacha obligingly lifted up one hind leg, exposing the milk bar. The baby got the idea and within seconds latched on to a teat, sucking with all her strength. This milk full of colostrum would protect the calf and build up her immune system, an absolute necessity for survival.

As the calf suckled, Tacha lay there patiently. Every now and then she raised her head to look around her and then settled back into the shallow water. A hippo's head is one of the heaviest parts of its body, partly due to the number of teeth in a fully grown animal's mouth: 36 in total, and some of them, like the lower canines in a big male, can be over a metre in length. Although their heads are weightless in the water, on land hippos take every opportunity to find a convenient pillow. Tacha, while remaining vigilant, was lying comfortably on her side in the shallow water, just deep enough for the baby to be submerged up to her little belly; and after her feed, the baby moved to a tiny sand island right next to them. Her wobbly gait was a joy to behold; she looked more like a puppy than a hippo, or perhaps like a seal. She lay down on the sand to sleep next to her mum.

I was so enthralled filming that I had for the moment forgotten the crocodile, so when it popped up in the water right behind Tacha's bottom it really startled me. But what happened next was even more surprising. Suddenly Tacha's afterbirth began to be ejected, and to my utter astonishment the crocodile plunged forward, grabbed a large piece of the placenta in its jaws, yanked it away and promptly began eating it. Tacha did not even stir. It was as if this was quite normal behaviour and the naturalist in me wondered if maybe it was. Perhaps this just happened to be the first time I had witnessed it. I knew that some people eat their own placenta or part of it, as it's supposed to help balance their hormones; but the crocodile's reaction suggested that this was a sought-after delicacy, because it was soon back, yanking more placenta out of Tacha's body.

As I began to film this extraordinary event the camera's battery ran dead and I knew that if I ran back to our home to charge the battery it would take too long and all the action would be over. So I just stood and watched in amazement.

The crocodile continued to feed and then yanked a particularly large lump of afterbirth out of Tacha. At that moment the tiny calf moved nearer to Tacha's hindquarters where the crocodile was feasting. Tacha's reaction was instantaneous: from her recumbent position she whipped around, lunging at the croc. Perhaps the predator was just that little bit too close to her calf. The crocodile did not budge at all, for it was too busy ripping at the massive lump of afterbirth. Tacha, now on her feet, lowered her gigantic head, opened her jaws, picked up the crocodile in her mouth and threw it up in the air. With a loud splash it fell back into the river at a distance from mother and baby.

I was stunned, and I cursed that I couldn't film this incredible behaviour. The crocodile was not in the slightest bit fazed by what had just occurred. It resurfaced with the placenta still clamped tightly in its jaws and swam away with its prize.

I was so excited by what I had witnessed that I could hardly wait to see Jean-Roger once he came home that evening. He had left early in the morning, accompanying the rangers on an anti-poaching patrol. Events like witnessing the dramatic introduction of a new hippo calf (we named her Bonbon) to her watery world made my life more than interesting; it filled up my entire day with excitement and, if possible, deepened my fascination with these amazing animals.

Bonbon's near catastrophic first taste of life was one of many incidents over the years that I am privileged to have shared. I still find it absolutely staggering the way the hippos appear to accept me into their lives. I suppose they are so used to having me around and hearing me talk to them that I am a kind of fixture in their wild existence; but what never ceases to surprise me is how these animals have allowed me to witness such intimate scenes at very close proximity.

Hippos have a bad reputation as one of Africa's biggest killers of humans. However, having observed these giant mammals at their gentlest and most vulnerable, and understanding their need to protect themselves, I reject this unjustified reputation. Hippos avoid humans as best they can but, being dependent on water during the daylight hours (although they may lie on sandbanks in the sun, especially during the winter months), they cannot abandon their watery habitat and easily find an alternative space. If people get too close to hippos when in boats or when washing at waterways, conflict can easily arise, particularly when hippo mothers have young calves and are feeling vulnerable and defensive.

People, too, are dependent on water. Those who use natural pools or rivers for recreation or washing are inevitably at risk if there's a hippo pod nearby. Some people are known to throw rocks at hippos, or use catapults to scare them away. Animals that are frequently exposed to such treatment, and which are large enough and able to attack are likely, at some stage, to retaliate. Having to share our habitat with that of wild animals requires our respect and understanding for the natural order of things.

12

Lions and wild dogs

Most of our volunteers and even local Zimbabweans seem to think that the lion is one of the most dangerous animals to come across in the bush when on foot. Yet, living here and having met lions on many occasions, both Jean-Roger and I tend to disagree. Lions that attack people are either in some way injured or very old – they are unable to hunt their normal prey, and so are looking for something easy and potentially defenceless. Or a mother with cubs may see people as a threat to her family, although her first instinct would be to get the cubs away from potential danger. In general, it would be a lion's last resort to attack a human. As with most wildlife, lions know that humans are the most dangerous predators of all, and so they tend to run away from intruders in their habitat, or avoid them as best they can. Lions and almost all wild animals will, nine times out of ten, warn you with a growl or a grunt that they are around; or, in the case of an elephant, the breaking of a branch – their particular way of telling you to back off.

Four incidents of such lion behaviour stand out in my mind. One was when Jean-Roger was on a patrol with the rangers – as always, they were on foot. Jean does not carry any weapon, while the rangers have only their wooden sticks. They were walking in the Turgwe riverbed and as they rounded a right-angled bend in the river they saw just ahead of them, perhaps 10 metres away, five lionesses on a waterbuck they had only just killed – they hadn't even taken their first bite. On seeing the men, the cats all stared and then grunted a bit, but they didn't leave the carcass. Jean and the rangers just backed away and took a different route so that they could continue along the river but without being too close to the lions.

On their way back from the patrol Jean decided that it would be a good time to comb the thick mopane forest for snares set between trees, as the lionesses would be safely occupied with their waterbuck meal. Halfway into the area a loud growl-grunt stopped them all short. Probably about 12 metres to their right they saw a large male lion. So once more they backed off and the lion just watched them go. He had warned them of his presence and they had reacted in the correct way, so no harm had befallen anyone.

On another occasion Jean had joined me to go and see the hippos. Kuchek's family at that time were about three kilometres from the house. We took the vehicle as we didn't have the time to walk there and back. After watching the hippos for a while we climbed up the riverbank to take a different route back to the vehicle. We were about 100 metres from the vehicle when I heard what I thought was a motorbike. No such vehicle should be in that area. We stopped to listen and figure out where it was coming from, worrying that it might be poachers. Some of them do have motorbikes, but they don't normally use them when poaching in our area.

The noise seemed to be getting louder – and then I saw her. Crouched near a thick bush was a lioness, and the noise we had heard was no motorbike: it was her, and she was not a happy kitty! We froze; then, using hand signals, I pointed her out to Jean, and nodded in the direction of the vehicle, suggesting that we just keep walking towards it.

The lioness's tail was not swishing, but she was angry; her eyes were tight and cold. She then stood up and we could see that she was a very big lioness. As we walked, she walked too, parallel to us. This had never happened to me before, so I was puzzled. She was not elderly – far from it – she was a beautiful animal. I was not too alarmed as the vehicle was fairly nearby. She walked with us the entire way to the Land Cruiser, but she was no longer growling. She was just extremely watchful of us, as we were of her. When we reached the vehicle she veered off to the left, and once we were inside I suggested we slowly follow her.

With a bit of bundu bashing (as it's called here, meaning to drive off the road or track and into the veld), we followed her. She did not seem particularly upset by this, but she walked with purpose. Then she stopped and began peering intently at one thickly grassed spot. And then I saw them: three small cubs, possibly around two months of age, popping their heads out from the long grass. She padded into the long grass and then must have squatted down with her cubs, as all four completely disappeared.

I didn't want to disturb her, especially as she had no back-up females or a male with her that we could see, so we drove away and headed back home. No wonder she had issued such a warning and walked along beside us, almost as though she were escorting us out of her area.

I did manage to get a couple of good photos of her and one of the cubs, but mainly of their ears. With her motorbike noise, that lioness had been warning us in no uncertain terms that she was around, but not once did she charge or show aggression; it was simply a warning to us to stay away.

Another time I was coming home alone from the hippos, having walked the six kilometres there and back, and was quite close to the house, just near the hippo pan that we had built for the hippos in the 1992 drought.

I had just reached the pan – which we still kept operational in case of another severe drought, pumping water into it from the Turgwe River – when a movement attracted my attention and I saw not more than 10 metres away a young male lion. He was just on the other side of the pan and staring intently at me. I stopped and couldn't resist taking a couple of photos of him, but then I realised that he really was paying me a lot of attention. There was no malice in his eyes or posture, just total curiosity – but then I do not really blame him. It had been raining when I left home, and I was wearing a blue poncho with red cherries on it; not really appropriate for the bush, but at least it kept the rain off me and my camera equipment. The poncho went right down to my ankles and the lion must have wondered what on earth this strange creature was.

I backed off, still facing him, until I was a little further away. Then, slowly, I turned and carried on towards the house. He started following me initially, but then he chickened out and just squatted and watched me go. Yes, when this happens, we respond as any human would; and of course the adrenalin kicks in and your mouth goes dry, but this is also a lot to do with excitement. A lion is a huge animal, made up mainly of muscle, and when you meet one on foot it's a pretty impressive sight.

The last incident concerned the lioness and her three cubs that I had met with Jean-Roger. I met them again in the bush. This time I was alone and it happened very quickly. It was nearly dusk and I was hurrying to get home as Jean was not there and it's not wise to walk at night in the bush, specially if you don't have a torch.

To my right, a running beige shape appeared. I realised it was a cub and it shot by in front of me and headed to my left at speed. I raised the camera, hoping for another cub, and sure enough, I caught half of the next cub's body as it dashed past to join its sibling. I then realised that they were probably either running to their mother, or that she would be following them. I also guessed that there would probably be a third cub to come: and so there was. He was more confident and wasn't running so fast, and I caught a relatively good photo of him. Then I saw, to my left, their mother. The cubs had been running to her. Neither she nor the cubs had made any sounds that I had heard, but the cubs knew exactly where she was. At all times she had been watching me, without approaching or in any way alerting me to her presence. I knew that her three cubs were now safely with her, so I continued along the path homewards, and nothing more happened. Again, my heart was thumping, but a happy thumping, if that makes sense.

Another predator that we have aplenty in this Conservancy is the endangered painted wild dog. At last count there were over 100 animals in eight different packs. A couple of volunteers from Europe, Neleke and Eveline, were with me when an amazing sequence of events unfolded.

Late one afternoon I took the volunteers to visit Kuchek's family of hippos, leaving the vehicle parked above the riverbank – exactly in the area where Jean and I had met the lioness we thought was a motorbike. We climbed down the riverbank and crossed a sandy beach and some rocks to get closer to the river, so that I could introduce them to Kuchek and his family. To stand just a few metres away from a family of hippos is very special, and something not many people have ever done.

As I by now knew all the hippos and their unique characters, having studied them from the time of their birth, I have an amazing relationship with them; they even tolerate and trust having other people visit, as long as they are with me. We had been standing with the hippos, who had put on a great show: two calves were playing in the water and then Kuchek gave some lovely wide-open gapes. As we turned to leave, an impala ran past us at speed, and the next second three wild dogs appeared not more than seven metres from us, intent on catching and killing the buck. Within seconds it was all over, the impala was dead, the three dogs had begun feeding and, in spite of their being so close to us, they were unfazed by our presence.

Neleke asked if we were safe, knowing that I did not carry any kind of weapon; but I know how wild dogs behave and could reassure her that it was okay as long as we didn't approach the dogs, just remained still and let them feed. While we were photographing and videoing I heard a rustle and to my utter astonishment I saw a huge crocodile, about three-and-a-half metres long, leaving the river and beginning to move towards the dogs and their kill. Crocodiles' eyesight and their sense of smell are probably among the best of any species, and clearly this individual knew meat was available, and wanted his share.

When the volunteers saw the croc they must have moved slightly, probably in fear, and that was enough to stop the croc in his tracks. He spun around and raced back into the river so fast I couldn't even catch a photo.

In the few minutes we had been there, the dogs had despatched most of the impala, with only bits of bone and the head and legs remaining. They then moved off and ran up the bank, the same path we were about to take. Dusk was approaching and I was aware that if our lioness was in the area she could easily smell the kill, and it wouldn't be sensible to hang around.

I started leading the volunteers up the bank when we heard the whooping sound that the dogs make when they are calling to the rest of the pack. To our excitement, the entire pack appeared above the riverbank and then ran down the path and past us as if we weren't there. I was astonished as 21 dogs ran past us, not more than a metre away.

I suggested that we go back down for a few more minutes to try to get some last photos of the entire pack, as this was such a special thing to happen. At the bottom of the slope two hooded vultures were already on the remains of the kill and all the dogs were excitedly chirping and making their happy sounds as they dashed around looking for bits of meat. As we stood watching in awe, three dogs approached us, stopping perhaps a metre away. I told the girls to freeze and stay very quiet and I did not even try to take a photo. One dog gave a small growl – just a warning – and then they turned and went to join their family. It was so special.

Those dogs are such powerful hunters and if there are enough of them, can take down even a large antelope, though they tend to stick to smaller buck like impalas, duikers, bushbuck and warthogs. They can dispatch their prey in record time. It would be so easy for a pack of dogs to kill a human, but I have never heard of their being aggressive and attacking people.

This experience, as well as the video and photos that I got, was one of the most special highlights of our time here. I think both the volunteers realised that it wasn't an ordinary occurrence, and how extremely lucky they were to have been part of it all. People have often seen wild dog kills, but to be on foot within metres of the pack when it happened, and also have the crocodile appear – well, that beats almost everything!

13

Little things can kill you

One question that our volunteers always want to know is how dangerous the hippos and some of the other animals are. I tell them that it's really not the big guys that they need to worry so much about, it's the little ones. We tell them on arrival as I show them the cottages where they will be sleeping that they must always shake out their clothes and, if possible, put everything away in cupboards or suitcases. For those who are tidy this is not a problem but, to persuade those who are a little slack, we often end up having to tell them about some of the incidents that have befallen us at home. And the bad guys are often the smallest of creatures!

One day Jean-Roger walked into the pantry wearing his slops, then suddenly let out an almighty screech. He came out shouting, 'Bring me the lavender oil!' That could mean only one thing: scorpion! This, though, was no ordinary scorpion but the king of scorpions, the Parabuthus, which, if you have an allergic reaction to its poison, can kill you. And even if it doesn't kill you, it will cause you pain way over the average bearable threshold.

After stinging Jean's foot, it had scuttled under a tin on the floor of the pantry. Now he was frantically dabbing the side of his foot with lavender oil. This is usually a miracle cure for most insect stings and snake bites. I went back into the pantry armed with a sheet of stiff paper and a glass to catch the offender and release it into the bush.

I found the culprit, which was enormous, and managed to put the glass over it and then slide the piece of paper under it. I took the trapped scorpion outside and deposited it far away from the house in a clump of bushes near some rocks under which scorpions love to bury themselves.

I returned to find Jean sweating and in excruciating pain. I made him lie on the sofa and raise his foot, as that often helps to ease pain, but not in this case. He was hurting badly and I was becoming increasingly concerned.

Earlier that year two other people in the area had been stung. The Whittalls were born in these parts, so they are hardened to most of what Africa can throw at one, but until then, no-one in their household had ever been stung by a Parabuthus. The first victim was Debbie, Roger and Anne's eldest daughter, who is a mother herself, and used to the ups and downs of living in the bush. She had stood on a Parabuthus at their photographic safari camp and had to be rushed to hospital as not only had the pain been beyond bearable, but her tongue had begun to swell in reaction to the scorpion's sting.

She had spent nearly four days in hospital and everyone had been terribly worried, but she had survived. Not more than a month later, Anne, her mother, had been stung and she, too, ended up in hospital. She told us later that she would rather give birth to all of her four children over again than have the pain of the sting – it was far worse than any childbirth she had gone through.

Jean-Roger was trying to act cool, but I was afraid. The nearest hospital, at Triangle, which is a very tiny setup, was over a three-hour drive away. If he passed out or became incapable of walking he would be far too heavy for me to lift and get into one of our vehicles. The rangers were all on their days off and Silas is even smaller than I am. I begged Jean to come with me to the hospital, but he refused.

Neither of us goes to doctors or hospitals unless we feel close to dying, as we prefer in most cases to self-diagnose and sort ourselves out, using either natural medication or, if it has to be drugs, perhaps a light antibiotic. We always keep a course of anti-malaria pills in the house for us and the staff but, sadly, for scorpions there isn't really any kind of cure, just painkillers and the hope that you are not allergic to their poison.

Jean continued to suffer and I to worry. It was now night-time and his pain was getting worse, which is always the case when you are sick; the evenings seem to make you feel far worse. Eventually listening to his moans became unbearable, with my mind jumping from one grim scenario to another.

I put the generator on, waited for the satellite dish to kick in and Whatsapped Debbie, who lives seven hours away in Harare. (We cannot make ordinary phone calls from home as there is no signal, but we can use Whatsapp on the Internet.) I knew it was pointless contacting Roger and Anne as they would be in bed, as would Roger's sister Jane be. So Debbie was my only hope. She had been stung by the same kind of scorpion and I trusted that she would be able to talk some sense into Jean.

She tried but, as with me, persuading Jean to seek medical help was like knocking one's head against a brick wall. So then I asked her for Butch's Whatsapp number. He is the husband of another of the Whittalls' daughters, Jenny. He was staying over at Humani at the time and I reckoned should still be awake. He answered and I explained what had happened. He told me that he and Charlie, Roger's manager, would come over and talk some sense into Jean, and so I waited. One hour later they arrived and verbally laid into Jean, saying if he got worse, which could easily happen, as had been the case with Debbie, I would never manage to help him get to the vehicle, so he had to stop being pig-headed and let me drive him to the hospital. Well, it worked – he agreed!

The men left and Jean hobbled to the truck with me trying ineffectually to support his weight. But I got him into the vehicle, told him to sit tight and off we went. Three hours later we arrived at Triangle and, needless to say, there seemed to be no one around. We finally found a nurse, the only one who appeared to be on duty, as it was now nearly 11 p.m. The hospital is very small, with only four private rooms that we, as members, are allowed to use and had done so on a couple of occasions with very bad malaria and a spider bite. The ordinary wards, which can take perhaps 40 people, are reserved for the staff and management of a huge sugar corporation from South Africa.

The nurse took Jean's blood pressure and her eyes nearly popped out of her head. It was sky high because of the pain he was in. She offered to give him an injection of painkiller, but again he refused, as he loathes injections. So she gave him a couple of pills and admitted him, saying that I, as his wife, could take the bed next to him. Jean couldn't sleep but there was nothing more the nurse could do for him until the doctor arrived. She had rung him and he had asked her a couple of questions and told her he would see Jean at 5 a.m. when he came on duty. That meant several more hours to go before the doctor would arrive.

Jean was cross with me, saying coming to the hospital was a waste of fuel and wear and tear on our vehicle on the bush roads, as nothing had helped him so far, including the dose of painkillers which were not having the desired effect. I told him to wind his neck in, as at least he was here and not at home if things became more difficult to cope with. I managed to fall asleep, but Jean did not: the pain was just too much, although he refused to have any more drugs and spent a very uncomfortable night. In the morning the doctor told him that he would be fine; that yes, his blood pressure was far too high, but that was understandable with such severe pain. He said it was unlikely any further complications would set in as they had done with Debbie, as by now the symptoms would have shown up. But he told Jean that if he insisted on going home, he must rest, as walking around would aggravate the situation and the pain, and that it would then take longer to recover.

By 7 a.m. we were back in the vehicle and on our way home, but at least my mind was at peace, knowing that Jean wouldn't have some serious setback. Now it was all a question of waiting. It took five days for the pain to lessen enough for Jean to be able to walk properly and feel himself again. Our respect for those tiny little creatures had increased tenfold. To date, we'd both been stung by the lesser scorpions and after not more than a day we were usually back to normal. I fervently hoped, then and now, never to be stung by a Parabuthus.

This story would, funnily enough, make even the most untidy of volunteers hang up their clothes and start shaking towels and shoes and suchlike. We had a similar but funnier story where nobody got hurt, but it could have been far worse. Before the hospital incident Jean got into the bath one night and felt something scratchy by his balls. He lifted it out of the water and, to his horror, saw it was a scorpion – and a bad one. He flung it onto the floor, from where I rescued and removed it. This was way before the later experience, but can you imagine what that kind of pain could have been like in such a delicate place! What was a scorpion doing in the bath, you may well ask. Well, we live in the bush. The roof of the house is thatched, except for in the bathroom and kitchen, where it's asbestos with a ceiling made of local matting. Scorpions like to get into crevices and dark places, such as the matting ceiling. This means they often end up falling into our bath or, at times, onto our bed, so one always checks before going to bed. The joy of living in the African bush!

So that I shouldn't be entirely outdone by Jean's experience, another type of little 'nasty' decided to bite me. In my case it was a violin spider. I had been walking in the riverbed in sandals and it was not until that night that I felt an itchy bite on the side of my ankle. Stupidly, I began to scratch at it, not knowing at the time that this is the worst thing you can do with a violin spider bite. It had appeared harmless, just a small spot, but as soon as I scratched it the toxins became irritated, and then the fun began. It started quite slowly with just pain in the ankle, but within a very short time the pain increased and started spreading up my leg. Finally the leg began to go a nasty shade of blue. I knew then that I was in trouble.

I was alone at the time as Jean was away working. We had no means of communication, and if I wanted to contact him I had to drive over to Humani and use Jane Davies' phone. The problem was that by this stage I couldn't put pressure on my foot and my leg was aching badly. In the end I had to send Silas on his bicycle to the safari camp seven kilometres away, where I knew they had a radio. He got there to find nobody about, but eventually a caretaker arrived, who had been fishing in the river. They radioed Humani and one of the workers at the Whittall's said he would let them know. Four or so hours later Hilton, one of Roger's professional hunters, arrived in his car. He found me with my leg up on a chair and I told him that I couldn't walk and didn't know what had bitten me, but that it was very sore; and it was obvious that my leg was not a pretty colour.

Being a big beefy fellow, he just scooped me up in his arms and carried me to the car. He drove me to Jane's house and helped me inside. Nobody was there either. I decided I should telephone Jean. As the phone connected all I got to say was, 'Hi, I have a problem …' and then I passed out. Evidently the poison was really beginning to kick in. By then Hilton had left, so I woke up on the floor, and I heard Arthur, Jane's husband, saying, 'Karen, what the hell are you doing lying on our carpet? Haven't you got your own carpet to lie on?' Arthur was known for his sarcastic humour.

I was not in a laughing mood. As I explained why I was lying on the carpet, Jane and another lady – thankfully a nurse – came into the room. When Jane suggested I take a bath, thinking that it would relax me and help with the pain, the nurse was horrified. She said that a bath in hot water would be the worst thing with blood poisoning, which was apparently what was happening to my leg, and that I had to get to the hospital as quickly as possible.

I managed to call Jean again to let him know that our earlier conversation had been cut short when I passed out. Roger was very kind and asked another of his employees, Matthew, to drive me to Triangle, about two-and-a-half hours from Humani. At the hospital they admitted me after the usual tests. The doctor was there this time and he gave me two injections and said he would check on me later. Meanwhile, I had to keep my leg raised.

Matthew was not allowed to sleep in the bed next to mine, the nurse informing me in a very stern tone, 'This man is not your husband'. Luckily, there was a bed in the next room and it was empty, so at least he could have a good sleep that night. The following day the doctor cut into the bite and pushed out pus, as one would lance and empty an abscess. It hurt when he first cut into it, but once he released the pus the pain receded immediately; the relief was wonderful. I was then allowed to go home, but told to dress the wound every day, keeping it clean and watching it. He said that he would have preferred to keep me in for observation, but he knew the patient he was dealing with: both Jean and I had by now gained a reputation for not wanting to stay in hospital, and he knew that I also had animals to take care of. Luckily, perhaps also thanks to the amount of lavender oil that I had initially put on the bite, it did not scar or, worse, go necrotic, which is something that can happen with bites from violin and sac spiders. Yet again, a tiny little guy had caused tremendous pain and anxiety, although it could have been so much worse without the Whittalls' help.

I suppose that in the more than three decades that we have lived this lifestyle we have not come off too badly. I, too, was later stung by a small Parabuthus, which was bad enough, but I stayed at home and handled the pain with painkillers. At some point Jean also had a spider bite and went to hospital, and that time they made him stay there. Initially, they said he should stay for one week, but after five days they let him come home as the wound was healing nicely. The doctor said that violin spider bites can sometimes put you in hospital for as long as a month, so I suppose we both got off pretty lightly.

Funnily enough, the very worst injury or ailment that I have ever had in the bush, other than malaria, was from one of our pussycats. We have six rescue cats now: Teddy, Amber, Lucky, Pretty, Nelson and Tinkerbell. Four are from an SPCA shelter and two from a farm that was taken over during the land invasions, with many animals killed or about to be killed.

Teddy is a ginger tom, a thick-bodied hairy thug with a heart of gold towards humans, but who hates with a passion any other cat, barring his pretty girlfriend, who is a tortoiseshell called Amber. Even with her, he occasionally has to have a rough and tumble, but in general they get along fine. He will not, though, tolerate any of the others and tries to kill them, so we have had to separate them. Our mongoose Squiggle regarded our house as her territory and would likely attack any new, unfamiliar cat that entered her domain. Her teeth were extremely sharp and if she attacked a cat, it might retaliate, with disastrous results on either (or both) sides. As a result, the cats were housed in two of the volunteers' cottages: Teddy and Amber together in one, and the other four in a separate dwelling.

I had a habit of letting the group of four cats outside in the morning, and then inside they would go after lunch, and out would come Teddy and Amber for the rest of the day. At night they all had to be safely inside, otherwise they risked being killed by predators such as owls. So everyone got to feel sunshine on their fur and play in the grass and meet all the other animals during the daytime.

One afternoon I didn't see Teddy lurking behind a wall near the other cats' cottage, and as I opened the door to go in, Pretty, one of the females, shot past me. Teddy leapt on to Pretty, biting and scratching her. Without thinking, I used my foot to try to push him off her. In his rage, Teddy attacked my foot and leg. He bit me in four places on my ankle, but at least I managed to push him outside and slam the door shut, stopping his attack on Pretty. Although the wounds were bleeding, I was so used to cutting my legs on thorn bushes that I thought nothing much of it; and, initially, I felt no pain. So I just washed the wounds, put on a bit of lavender oil and got on with my day.

Teddy was by now back to his loving self with me, and behaving as if nothing at all had happened. Later that night the pain set in. By the morning I couldn't put pressure on my foot and none of the four wounds looked great. We phoned a doctor in Harare whom we had consulted once before. She was not keen to diagnose on the phone, but after we explained that driving seven hours just for an appointment was not really what we wanted to do, she capitulated. She asked us what antibiotics we had at home. We only had one kind, and she told me to take a course of those.

Three days later my whole leg was swollen and the wounds were red and ugly. When we phoned the doctor again, she said that obviously those antibiotics were not appropriate, and suggested we try another kind that she said should solve the problem. To buy this new medication required Jean's driving to Chiredzi, a four-hour drive there and back. Concerned by the sight of my leg, he dutifully did just that. On his return I started on the second course of antibiotics. This second round of medication was particularly unwelcome for a person who doesn't normally take any kind of drugs other than the odd over-the-counter paracetamol.

This had happened at the worst time for me, as it was December, the busiest month for working online. During this period the Turgwe Hippo Trust is extremely busy with people either purchasing one of the calendars that I sell annually, or adopting a hippo. I often work around 12 hours a day online, especially on Christmas Day and Boxing Day, but the monies that come in during that period can, if we are lucky, cover the Trust's expenses for up to three months, bar any emergencies needing extra funds. I also need to keep communication flowing for hippo 'adoptions': each adoptive customer receives five emails with attachments such as photos and videos, along with individual certificates. Many of those people adopting hippos remain virtual friends but I have also had the pleasure of meeting and becoming real-life friends with some of them. They tell me they love the personal touch my emails bring. So it's worth the full-on effort at that time of the year.

Unfortunately, the new antibiotics were not making any difference either as the pain and the swelling were continuing and, if anything, increasing. In the end I contacted a friend in Australia who is a nurse and told her what had been happening. I gave her the name of the two antibiotics and asked her if there was any chance she could speak to one of the doctors at her hospital and ask their opinion. Karlene was amazing. She got back to me on Facetime, saying the doctor had suggested an entirely different antibiotic as he believed the ones I had taken to date were inappropriate. I couldn't have agreed more.

So off Jean drove again to Chiredzi and, much to our amazement, he found the pills in one of the only two chemists in the town. Karlene's instructions were that I should stop the second lot of antibiotics, wait one day, and then start the latest batch.

By now I was entering the second week since Teddy had bitten me, and the pain was as bad as ever. I was constantly applying a wet or icy cloth to my leg in an effort to ease the pain – the cold seemed to help a bit. Once I was on the new pills I noticed a change very quickly. The swelling went down and within two days my leg had returned to normal, and the bites, though still visible, were not as red. I could at last put my foot down on the floor without feeling pain.

Yet again, one little guy, a fluffy orange pussycat, had put me out of action, and this time for even longer than the spider or the Parabuthus scorpion. If a cat can give such infection with its bite, then I hate to think what a lion bite must be like – that is, if you haven't been entirely eaten in the first place!

14

An earthquake and a meteor

I don't know if living in a natural environment surrounded by vast open spaces, trees, rivers and sky makes significant natural events seem even bigger and more dramatic, but this is my impression, especially when one is alone in the bush and cannot ask a nearby neighbour what their experience was like. One such occurrence happened in the middle of the night. At around two in the morning I was woken by a very loud roaring together with a powerful vibration so that it felt as if the entire house was about to collapse. This was unlikely as Jean-Roger had built our home using rocks for the walls, strongly cemented in place. I hoped that the deep foundations supporting the entire building would withstand whatever was happening.

At first I wasn't sure if I was dreaming; but soon I was convinced that the house really was vibrating. My first thought was that an elephant was in the front garden and, for some peculiar reason, was shaking our thatched roof at one of the corners where it dipped downwards. Should I go out and shout at him? The rumbling and roaring increased, and then all the cats (which lived in the main house at that time, as we did not then have Squiggle) rushed towards the living area and the front door, wanting to get out – something they had never before wanted to do at night. I had to wake Jean who was still, as always, sleeping like a baby. As soon as his eyes were open he knew exactly what was going on and his geological training kicked in.

'Earthquake!' he shouted. 'Get out of the house now!'

Luckily, it was during the cooler months of winter and I was wearing a nightshirt as I rushed out of the door, along with four petrified cats. I had no idea what to do. I felt as if I was in a movie, and that at any moment the earth would crack open and we would fall into some deep and dark crevice. It was terrifying. Jean yelled that I should get away from any building or tree and he would quickly go to the rangers' and Silas's homes and make sure they, too, were out of their buildings.

He found all six men outside in their underpants, with wide staring eyes, frightened to death. Silas asked Jean, 'Is God coming?' Jean patted him on the shoulder, telling him it would be okay, it would be over soon.

The bush was silent, there was not a single animal or bird noise, just the rumbling and shaking still carrying on. Inside the house, however, I could hear things crashing off the bookshelves and I really expected to see the house disappear into the ground. I kept remembering all the disaster movies I had watched on DVDs. Afterwards, Jean told me that he had held on to our mopane wooden staircase as we made our way out of the door and that even that solid hardwood structure was throbbing.

The entire episode lasted for over 15 minutes, and then there were four aftershocks over the next couple of hours. The next day when we could connect up to the Internet we learnt that the quake had registered over seven on the Richter scale, which is rather high. The only apparent structural damage at our home was a crack that now ran through the cement and ochre finish in our living-room floor but, as Jean-Roger remarked, it gave the house an attractive, somewhat vintage look. A few ornaments were broken, but luckily none of my special ones.

At neighbouring Humani they were worse off as their homes were built entirely with local bricks, and huge cracks had opened up in many of the walls. An entire garage had collapsed, but luckily nobody had been hurt. It certainly was a talking point for the rangers, who were to discover when they went home on leave that it had also affected their own properties. It had been felt as far away as Harare, but not to the same level as we had experienced it. The epicentre had been in Mozambique and, fortunately for the people there, it happened way out in the middle of the bush, with hardly any homes or people around, so again, very little damage had been done.

For one who likes to be in control of her life, Nature had dramatically awoken me to the insignificance of human beings on the global geological scene. The behaviour of the birds and animals had been fascinating: even though this happened in the pitch dark when most of the animals should have been sleeping, once the aftershocks were over it was as if dawn had suddenly lit up the sky. In the distance we heard elephants trumpeting and the hippos calling, not just one or two but a whole family calling to each other; and the birds and insects sang and chirped. Absolutely nobody was silent, so I think they too, like us, had had quite a big scare.

A few years after the quake Jean-Roger and I were away for two nights in the fantastic wilderness area called the Gonarezhou, the National Park nearest to our home. When Squiggle was with us, we never went away for more than three nights, and normally only two, as we didn't like to leave our mongoose on her own. At such times Silas would sleep in the house in the living area on a camp bed alongside Squiggle's large cage. She would never allow him to handle her but at least he could keep an eye on her, and keep her food and water topped up. When we got home Silas came rushing towards us and my heart for a moment nearly ceased beating. My immediate fear was that something had happened to Squiggle, but Silas saw my face and hastened to assure me that all the animals were fine. I speak only a tiny bit of a mixture of Shona and Ndebele, and Silas, who has never been to school, speaks pidgin English. Between us, with a lot of hand signals, we communicate. Now he described what had happened the previous evening, and these are the words he used:

'I was in the house, it was dark no moon, then it began a noise, and the sky was on fire. It became light like when the rains come, when the white light happens with the large bangs, but it was not the same. All around was a kind of long tail like a baboon's, but made of light. It was moving like a car but much bigger and at the end of it looking like at the workshop on Humani when they use the welding machine, the sky was all like that. It moved fast past our houses and over to Chlabata, then there was a big bang and it went dark again. I was not happy, Squiggle and the cats were not happy, the rangers were not happy, but it did not come back.'

Jean-Roger yet again knew what it was: a meteor. From Silas's description it had fallen pretty close by, which was very exciting: meteorites, or bits thereof, can be worth a lot of money. I was thinking, whoa, I could stop fundraising for many years and the Trust and the hippos and other animals would be okay. Wouldn't it be great if we could find some valuable rocks? Jean was thinking the same way, so we checked quickly on the animals, telling Silas he would be fine and we were going to see what had fallen out of the sky. We got back in the vehicle and drove over to the area where something had allegedly crashed to earth.

Jean and I spent about three hours battling through thick spiky bushes and reeds, searching for a crater or some kind of disturbance, but we found nothing at all. And eventually we gave up the search. Jean felt sure that it had not landed in our immediate area, but that, to Silas, it had just sounded very close. We came back to the house with bleeding legs and arms from the branches and thorns, and nothing valuable to show for it at all.

We found out afterwards that we were not the only ones who had gone searching for the meteorite. Bryce and Lara Clemence run the extremely efficient anti-poaching tracking unit 50 kilometres to the north of us on Sango, the largest property within the Conservancy. They safeguard all the rhinos in the area, and they had also hoped to find a pot of gold at the end of the rainbow. So much so that Pete, Bryce's dad, and Bryce had driven all the way towards Chipinge, a few hours away, to where they thought it had fallen. They, too, had found nothing.

We read a week later that the meteor had landed in a farmer's field just on the other side of Chipinge, but we have never heard if anyone found the meteorite debris, and if they made their fortune out of it. Yet again, Silas and the rangers had quite a story to tell their wives and families when they returned home on their days off.

Other momentous natural events are flooded rivers and roads – all part of the territory when the rains arrive in the bush. In the years we have been here there have been many occasions in the rainy season on which we have not been able to leave our home for several days. This is when the dirt road out of our property can, for 12 kilometres, be completely awash, becoming too flooded and muddy to drive on even with a four-by-four vehicle. Once one reaches the main Conservancy dirt road it's easier to drive out towards the towns, but that depends on two rivers.

When the Turgwe River comes up during the rains it can rise so high that for up to two months it's impossible to cross, ruling out our heading north of the Conservancy to take the shorter route up to Harare, which is still a seven-hour drive away for us. If the Turgwe is too full, then there is an alternative river to negotiate, the Mkwasine River. It usually floods for a maximum of 24 hours, although we have had two cyclones in this area, and on those occasions we couldn't cross either river for over two months.

There are no shops here and no way of getting provisions, so we always keep as much stock as possible in our pantry for these kinds of situations. If we cannot drive out to collect drinking water, which we normally fetch once a week, then we collect rainwater and drink that – it's the nicest water to drink if you can keep it free of debris like leaves and insects. You make a plan, as they say in Zimbabwe, for all these events and just hope that the river, when in flood, does not wash away the cement causeways that facilitate crossing riverbeds by car. When that does happen, however, we are grateful to Roger Whittall at Humani who is usually burdened with getting the Turgwe causeway fixed, using his tractors, graders and bulldozer. We cannot help as all we have to fix our own roads are our hands and a wheelbarrow.

Floods can cause us problems, but most of the animals that live in the riverine areas or in the river, like the hippos, always seem to know beforehand that the river is going to flood, and so they leave the area. The hippos move to smaller rivers that do not hold water in the dry, but have flowing water when we get good rain. The buffalos and other animals that are often in the *Phragmite* reeds surrounding the river also move away before a flood arrives. The only animals that we have seen that can get caught out by floods are either small animals such as tortoises, perhaps carried away by a flash flood while crossing a part of the river that was initially dry, or the baboons.

On a few occasions our home troop of baboons has become stranded in the trees in which they roost at night. Trees growing within the riverbed shallows normally provide the baboons with safety from most predators, but when the river rises too much they become trapped.

The longest time I have seen baboons stuck in trees was, fortunately, only three days. It was awful to see them all high up in the canopies, having to wait for the waters to recede. Once they felt it was safe enough, they slowly, one by one, would climb down and then either leap from one tree to another, or to a rock that was no longer submerged. All the babies would cling tightly to their parents, confident that this would keep them out of harm's way. I have never seen even one of them fall into the rushing water.

During cyclones it's a different story. In such events the flooding of the rivers has been very bad, especially in the 2000 cyclone when many animals did perish. I had at that time 33 hippos, and nine of them disappeared, never to return. I heard many years later that five of them had moved to an area where resident land invaders had shot them for meat. Again, another part of my heart is cut away but I have to move on and hold with the thought that I am making a difference, and be thankful that cyclones do not happen too regularly.

15

Elephant mishap

We share our lives with most of Africa's wildlife. In the Conservancy, which covers a huge area of around 1,500 square kilometres, there are supposedly over 1,200 elephants. Normally the herds consist of around 25 animals at most, but at certain times of the year these herds may join up with others, and in our area it's not unusual to see up to 100 elephants moving together, like one big family.

Elephants are the gardeners – even the landscapers – in Africa, and some people regard these huge mammals as having a negative impact on the African environment. I take the opposite stance: nothing in Nature is destructive. Animals, insects and birds all have a part to play, and all complement one another.

Elephants need trees, not only for their bountiful nutritious leaves but also to use for a really good bottom rub. And yes, elephants do break trees. If a tree branch is out of reach, it's obvious to the elephant to push the tree over, if it can. 'Destruction!' cry the opponents, proclaiming how terrible the land looks when many trees have been felled by elephants. Yet what happens once a tree goes down?

First of all, most tree breakage is done by elephants at the very driest time of the year, when almost all the animals are desperate for fodder. Once the tree is down, along come smaller animals that couldn't have reached the leaves the taller animals could browse, and that can now feed easily. I have watched a multitude of different browsing animals feeding from trees and branches broken by elephants. These felled trees create a new habitat for many species that normally would not have existed in a thickly wooded forest of mainly tall trees.

Often the tree doesn't die – many species have evolved to coppice, sending up several stems and branches from the felled trunk. Sometimes, from one tree, up to three new ones arise. They may never be as tall as that first tree, but this is how 'gardeners' work: they change landscapes to fit a pattern. Landscapes and their inhabitants evolve together.

Elephants are attracted to areas with a permanent water source, particularly in regions as dry and drought stricken as the Save Valley Conservancy. And because of their massive weight and strength, elephants do sometimes in their enthusiasm damage water infrastructure, but there are ways of protecting such structures, for instance with sturdy stone walls.

People who live at a distance from elephants tend to see them as gentle giants, which is justified to some extent where the elephant has been left in peace and not persecuted by humans, and whose living space has been respected. However, many who live in the vicinity of wildlife and who, worse, make their living from hunting animals, fear the larger species, especially the elephants. When they talk about an elephant it's never with joy or a light heart, it's always negative, filled with all the dark aspects of what they see.

Elephants can certainly kill people, and when they do it's not at all pretty. This is a huge animal with so much strength that, when angered, it can without a doubt be very dangerous. If elephants and their immediate family are constantly under threat and have witnessed severely stressful events, they develop a negative attitude towards humans. Usually their first instinct is to try to get away from people. I have known huge elephant bulls that I have been watching in the bush suddenly catch wind of my scent and, to my distress, run away from me. It's amazing how most large animals that could do away with us with just a flick of their trunk or snap of their teeth, or simply by virtue of their weight, run away from us.

To have four- or five-ton animals afraid of just the whiff of a human not only brings tears to my eyes and makes me ashamed to be part of the human race, but it also makes me exceedingly angry. This fear of our human scent can only be because of traumatic events in the lives of these incredibly intelligent animals. Or it's an inherited fear of humans who, going back to time immemorial, have killed any and all animals that have got in their way. Elephants have very long memories, as do hippos and many other animals (even the domestic cow, but that's another story). It's likely that the bulls that were disturbed by my scent had lost family members to hunters.

By the time the Save Conservancy was formed in 1991, only around 50 elephants remained in the area as ranchers had shot all the wildlife that interfered with their livelihoods. But as the cattle were removed and the ranching fences were taken down, the ranchers brought back wildlife from other areas which were often overstocked with one or other species. Among these animals translocated into the area were over 450 elephants.

The severe drought had also resulted in many elephants dying in the area, including in the Gonarezhou, the nearest National Park to the Conservancy. The elephants there had, over many decades, been decimated by sport hunters, poachers and even park staff members, and were notorious for their aggressive behaviour towards people, both on foot and in vehicles. Elephants had even been used as ration meat to feed the National Park staff – a practice now no longer tolerated by many parks. And, shockingly, the armies from South Africa and within Zimbabwe killed many elephants during the years of political upheaval.

At the time of the drought it was decided that, in order to save elephant lives, a few hundred of the animals should be translocated from Gonarezhou to the Conservancy. The UK animal charity, Care for the Wild, which had sponsored my feeding of the Turgwe hippos and was willing to fund the elephant translocation, had hammered out an agreement with the landowners of the Conservancy at that time regarding the elephants. In return for their funding, it was stipulated that no elephant could be shot for a minimum of 10 years, although they would have liked a much longer moratorium. After that, once the owners were allowed to hunt again, they could take five bulls per year for trophy hunters; plus, they were allowed to shoot so-called 'problem elephants' said to be raiding crops in the nearby communities if this were proven to be the case. From the beginning, Conservancy land owners were worried about the elephant population as they knew they would breed successfully; and, although there was hardly a sign of what is often called 'elephant damage' (broken trees and landscapes changed by elephant activity), they felt that they should still keep the numbers down by culling up to 60 elephants each year, as well as killing the 'problem' animals that cross out of the Conservancy and supposedly cause havoc in communities by raiding crops or even, very occasionally, injuring or killing someone.

The moratorium was observed, but once it had ended, and with sport hunting and culling taking place, we noticed the elephants' behaviour begin to change. They became nervous again, and at times aggressive as their memories from their Gonarezhou life resurfaced. Most of the landowners in this Conservancy run sport hunting safaris where, sadly, every year several elephants are legally shot by international hunters, mostly Americans, as long as they are accompanied by a trained professional Zimbabwean hunter. So the elephants in the Conservancy are afraid of humans.

This means that when I walk or drive in the bush in this area I can never be altogether relaxed with elephants, unlike in certain limited other areas of Africa where the hunting of any wildlife is prohibited, or where there is control and the poaching is minimal. There you will meet the legendary gentle giants, although, as with any wild animal, you cannot simply go up to them and pat them on the trunk. They are wild, huge and able to kill a human very easily, even if they don't intend to hurt us. With their immense size and strength it's easy for an irritated elephant to attack even a vehicle and smash it up badly, or turn it over and stomp on it.

Happily, many of the worst parks are now managed by outside organisations like the Frankfurt Zoological Society, including the entire Gonarezhou Park area, on which the Society has a long lease. They have ploughed money into the Park for improvements and for training their rangers, and the work they have achieved is miraculous. The rangers are under constant supervision and there are experts in the wildlife field supervising the anti-poaching units. Hunting in the park, which was always illegal but which was still being carried out before the takeover, often by the very people who were supposed to care for the animals, is now under control and poaching has been reduced considerably.

They no longer ration any wildlife for meat for their staff. Instead, they buy dried fish or meat either from commercial setups in the towns or elsewhere, but they do not kill the very wildlife they are committed to protecting – which is a much better way of setting an example to future generations of rangers and wildlife protectors. The Rangers we employ for the Turgwe Hippo Trust are also given only dried fish and rations that we buy in the local town; they are never given wild animal meat. One fantastic ranger setup near the Victoria Falls, run by an extremely forward-thinking Australian, employs only female rangers. This man has every ranger eating only vegan food!

Since the Gonarezhou's first association with the Frankfurt Zoological Society in 2007, near-miraculous improvements have taken place, including protection of the wildlife that has enabled the numbers of elephants, among many other species, to recover significantly. The elephants, once notorious for their aggressive behaviour towards people, both on foot and in vehicles, are beginning to calm down, and in the 12-plus years that we have been going there, we have seen a noticeable change in their behaviour. The elephant cow herds there can still be nervous, and if you do something unexpected or that appears threatening to them, they will react and can be very dangerous. But nowadays, if you are sensible in your approach, they tend to move off and not charge, as they often did in previous years.

Luckily, the droughts we have had since 1992 have not been too hard on the browse, so those animals that eat leaves, such as elephants, have been able to survive without my help. But hippos only graze and the grass in 2016 was nonexistent, so I had to step in, and for a longer period (14 months) than in the nineties before I could back away and leave the hippos to return to their normal lives without my intervention.

That year I had no fewer than 18 feeding stations out in the bush. I would spend from late morning until dusk taking food to all of them and making sure that each area had sufficient food not only for the hippos but also for any of the other wildlife that came along to feed. I was covering one area 14 kilometres away, where I had two hippos; another area three kilometres from home, feeding one family of hippos as well as many other wild animals; another area six kilometres from the house for all the wildlife and, of course, for the 16 hippos living in a pool at the end of the track. I was feeding 24 hippos and over 250 other animals – and then along came the elephants. Up until mid-September they had found only a couple of the stations and had investigated them, eating a few of the horse cubes but then moving on, as there was still plenty of browse available in the bush.

In the years of living here we have had one or two elephants give a small demonstration of their power by loud trumpeting or, now and again, a mock charge. But until 2016 I had never had a life-threatening encounter. My respect for these animals knows no bounds and, although my work here is primarily to try to sustain the Turgwe hippos in the face of anything that can hurt them, I feel as much love for the elephants.

The big elephant misadventure had to happen when my good friend Jill Robinson was staying with us. She is the founder of Animals Asia in China, their mission being mainly to save moon bears from the evil and cruel bear bile farming that takes place in China and Vietnam. Jill arrived in October, one of the hottest months, when we hope to have rainfall; but by about the middle of November the veld was extremely dry and lacking in colour. Like all who are caught by Africa's immense power over the senses, she was thrilled to be meeting many of the wild animals that I was feeding. She and the vet nurse who works alongside her, Wendy, accompanied me a couple of times to the feeding stations.

Jill and Wendy were in the vehicle that day in 2016. It was late afternoon and my Land Cruiser, 'Miss Sunshine' as she is called, being yellow in colour and a very old lady who still has a lot of power, was filled to the brim with hay and horse nuts as well as two rangers on the back of the truck sitting on the hay bales. Jill, Wendy and I were tucked up in the front; none of us are big women, so we could just fit in.

We were on our way to Tembia's family of hippos. Tembia, the son of Bob, is one of my special boys whose family has always been a larger pod than the other bulls'. Tembia and his family at that time constituted a bloat of 16 hippos, and I was feeding all of them every afternoon. This involved a drive of six kilometres upstream on roads that only my four-wheel-drive vehicle can reach.

The road, or should I say dirt track, is maintained only by us. It turns and twists, with narrow passages between very thick mopane forests, and undulates over steep stony ground surrounded by rock koppies. Along part of the route the mountain Acacia trees open up the landscape slightly, but then you return to the forests of mopane. It is certainly a four-by-four driver's dream; that is, if you like dropping down into sandy riverbeds, climbing back up steep rises and then manoeuvering along narrow tracks, somewhat like the small twisty lanes found in Cornwall in the UK – but without the smooth tarmac and comfortable hedges and laybys to accommodate cars coming in the opposite direction.

On this single, narrow bush track there are hardly any places in which to turn around, so I always have my heart in my mouth when driving up to the hippos at the Majekwe weir. If you do meet a herd of elephants, not only do they have right of way, but they can make your life a little nerve-wracking if they decide that the road belongs exclusively to them.

We had only just left home and were not more than five minutes away when I saw within the dry riverbed to the right of me, called the Chichindwi, a small herd of seven elephants milling around near the river's confluence with the Turgwe River. They were down below us, so not on the road. I stopped the vehicle so that Jill and Wendy could take some photos out of the windows, and then noticed that there was a tiny calf amongst the females, possibly even a newborn. It was extremely wobbly on its feet, although I couldn't see it clearly as it was partly hidden behind its mother.

The two rangers in the back were being very quiet: we all know that elephants in this area do not like the sound of human voices. As we watched the herd my attention was suddenly grabbed by the appearance of a female on the top of the opposite bank of the river. Within seconds she was charging down the slope and coming straight at us. Her head was down and she was not playing – this was one very angry elephant.

I had no option but to move the vehicle forward; to reverse would have been impossible before she would be on top of us. Besides, reversing a Land Cruiser is never that easy as they are not nimble vehicles, and to reverse uphill and around bends would have been just too slow. So I did what my instincts told me to do, and that was to put my foot down and move quickly forwards, hoping that she would stop before reaching our side of the riverbed. But we were not going to be let off that easily.

I took off as fast as I could on such a narrow, twisting route but she was already up on our side of the bank and coming up very fast behind the vehicle. The rangers were not happy as they were getting a full view of the irate elephant cow in full charge mode. They had been taught by us never to leave the vehicle in situations like this, and so they were clinging to the back of the Cruiser as I drove with as much speed as was possible in such a confined area. Jill was telling me what was happening as I had absolutely no time to look in the rear-view mirror; all my attention was focused on driving at speed in the impossibly confined space, the twisting and turning track thickly bordered on both sides with mopane trees. Jill was saying that the elephant was catching up, but I couldn't go any faster.

I was about to reach a place where I had to stop the vehicle as we would be going down a steep slope into the Chichindwi River which, although dry, is full of sand and I knew I would have to change to low range in order to get out of the sand and back up the steep opposite bank. Normally one does this very slowly and carefully, and I have to get out of the vehicle to change the locks on the hubs of the wheels, then put the vehicle gear stick into low range and slowly move down into the river and up the other side. This was not going to be a normal crossing, not with an enraged elephant in pursuit and about to catch us up.

As I stopped to change gears, silently thanking Jean-Roger who had put the hubs in lock before we left home (something I don't normally do), I realised it was too late to attempt crossing the riverbed. In a flash, both rangers appeared up front on the bonnet, fear written all over their faces. Thankfully, they had come to the front and not tried to run off into the bush. I knew the elephant was going to hit us, so I shouted to everyone to brace themselves as we were about to be hit by four tons of elephant. I was not sure if she would manage to turn us over. As I said 'Brace!' my foot slipped on the accelerator and the vehicle made a loud revving sound ... and nothing happened. No big thud or shaking of the vehicle. We had not been hit.

Both rangers were still hanging on to the bonnet and there was no time for them to return to the back, so I just slammed the vehicle into low range, shot down the slope and back up the other side in record time. Never had I driven my old vehicle at such a reckless speed, but foremost in my mind was that I was responsible for the safety of everyone. Once I realised that the cow was not following, that the emergency was over, I changed gear and announced that we would keep going in order to lay the food out for the hippos.

To say that all of us were a bit shaken-up is an understatement, but at all times everyone had remained quiet and not overtly panicked. I think working with bears in China had helped both Jill and Wendy, who knew how dangerous a large animal can be and were well aware that you have to keep your wits about you at all times, and try not to panic.

We had a problem, though. We had got away from the elephant, but this was the only road on which to return, and I was not sure if the herd would still be where we had found them earlier. I was determined to feed the hippos and so, with shaking hands, I continued driving up to the feeding stations, where we laid out the food. However, I could see that one of the rangers, Chengati, was not happy. He had left his previous employment because of an incident with an elephant. His employer had been driving around his ranch with Chengati when, like today, an elephant had charged them and in that case had hit the truck. Luckily, once it had assaulted the truck it backed off and after some time they could continue, albeit with a severely dented vehicle.

This now was his second experience, and although the elephant had not hit us, he told me that when they both leapt out and ran to the front of the vehicle, the elephant was within touching distance. They were incredibly lucky that she had not grabbed one of them. I wondered if he would quit the job. Peter, the other ranger, had never been charged before, and appeared not to be as upset as Chengati.

After laying out nearly a ton of hay along the route, plus the survival ration and horse cubes, it was time to return. I had no way of contacting Jean-Roger, as we do not have radios and there is no phone reception in our area. Besides, this was our only four-by-four vehicle, so it wasn't as if he could drive our way and see if the coast was clear. It was up to me, and I still had Kuchek hippo and all his family to feed near the house on our return. I just had to hope that if we got stuck with an elephant road block that Jean would go ahead and feed the hippos at home.

We set off homewards and as we reached the place near to the Chichindwi River I saw the herd. As I had feared, they had not left. This wasn't good. I felt we had been extremely lucky not to have been hit earlier, and to antagonise them by reappearing was perhaps a foolish thing to do. The rangers were in agreement, but now we had a second problem. The area is heavily poached by the land invaders, so if we had to abandon the vehicle and walk home, skirting the elephants, would Miss Sunshine still be in one piece the next day, or even there at all? Maybe the elephants would have a game with it. Yet I had no option. There were no other road tracks back to the house, and the route was too rocky, with large dry-river crossings, to drive home through the bush; no vehicle would make it. So we would have to walk.

By now dusk was descending, and to walk would mean around three kilometres through an area I knew was home to a pride of eight lions. Should I let Jill and Wendy know? We were not armed and all we had in the vehicle were the rangers' two machetes, which we use for cutting trees knocked down by the elephants that are blocking the tracks. I drove back about one kilometre then veered off into the bush and parked under a copse of trees, hoping we would find the vehicle again without any problems. I put the spare tyre into the locked cab and off we set.

112

I had Chengati take the lead, and then me, followed by the visitors, with Peter at the back of the single file. I was less worried about the lions than the elephants; if they moved from where we had left them, we could easily meet them on the round route we were taking, given the fast pace at which elephants can walk. I did not fancy seeing the angry cow again, with all of us on foot; but we had to get home so there was no alternative.

The walk was without incident, with no elephants and no lions, but I know that our visitors' hearts were beating loudly in their chests and their mouths were dry with apprehension – once the house came into view, they told me so. Several beers and a whisky or two later had them reliving every detail and also being very kind to me. Jill told me that I had been incredibly calm and collected and in charge. I said she had evidently not noticed my shaking hands.

Jean had been out, feeding Kuchek, so once I had the girls settled with their drinks, I joined him. He was just finishing laying out all the food and Kuchek and family had arrived and were standing near the river pool like well-behaved dogs. I told Jean what had happened and he was amazed as he thought we'd had a puncture. It had never crossed his mind that we might have had a much more serious setback. Probably just as well, as there would have been nothing he could have done.

So all ended well. We discussed it for a long time that night and all of us felt the same way: it was not at all the elephant's fault. Something bad must have happened to her or she had witnessed something terrible, and the vehicle and its human occupants had taken the brunt of her annoyance and fear. Luckily for us, and for her, she had not managed to do any damage. I do not believe her anger was due to the newborn calf and our close proximity to mother and calf. I have often met elephants with young calves and never had such a problem.

Once elephants have squared off against a vehicle and discovered how easy it is, they may repeat the assault. This could have made my life very difficult, having to go up there every day with the possibility of an angry elephant finishing off my vehicle. Worse still, she could have moved on to other properties where an elephant assailing a vehicle would mean retaliation, and she could easily have been shot.

Perhaps she was just having a very bad day and wouldn't have been like that on any other day. I had to continue feeding for at least another month or two until the main rains fell, and although each trip up there filled me with trepidation, I never did see her again. I think both she and we humans were lucky that day.

16

Steve hippo

During my life I have had the privilege of bonding with quite a few animals. I have lived with many different species but, for some reason, at every stage there has always been one animal that has stood out more than the others. You shouldn't really have favourites among people or animals, but I can't help it; now and again something exceptional occurs, and when it does it leaves an indelible memory. Steve, or Stevie as he prefers to be called, is one of these animals.

When male hippos are between two-and-a-half and three-and-a-half years of age they are normally chased out of the family group, especially if their mother is about to have a new calf. Daughters can stay with her – albeit at a distance from the new calf – but males are evicted. It's a tremendously traumatic time for a male hippo: these animals are naturally gregarious and are used to living a harmonious life not just with their mother but also with the entire family pod. A young male must find it hard to understand why, all of a sudden, he is not welcome, and even his mother turns on him. She becomes aggressive, refusing to let him suckle her milk and this weaning process often results in violence – she may attack him, especially if he resists leaving her. I have seen some young males with quite mean-looking slashes and cuts on their body, inflicted by their mother.

This is normal hippo behaviour. The males will grow up and eventually become threats to one another if there are limited areas for the hippos to live in. In most cases only one dominant bull can be in charge of a family of females and their young. Other male offspring, inevitably upcoming contenders for dominance, have to move out and find themselves somewhere to live far enough away from the family so as not to be attacked either by their own mother or, when they have matured, by the bull. Once a male has been chased away, the dominant bull, who is very often their father, will not allow it to return to the pod, and may even kill it.

In the years that I have lived with these hippos eight males have been killed by other hippos. The oldest one was nine years of age, but most of the others were mere juveniles, and one was even a young calf. Sadly, this happens not just among hippos, but among many other animals too. Most male animals, where there are family groups, have to leave the group and live either with other males or on their own.

In other areas of Zimbabwe I have even seen some male hippos living happily together, but it's usually in areas where the rivers are huge, like the Zambezi, so they can move away if territorial issues arise. The Turgwe River is not that wide and only 35 kilometres of its course run through the Conservancy. Once the river enters the community land, the presence of humans and harassment prevent hippos from settling there.

Steve was born in September 2017 and is now a juvenile male hippo; his mother is called Relief and his father is Kuchek, the bull living in the pools close to our home. Stevie was one of the hippos that I had to feed in the drought of 2019. As a calf, he came along with his family every night to the feeding station right near our house, a short distance from the riverbed. At that time he kept close to his mother, but he was rapidly reaching the age when he would have to leave the family.

The inevitable separation started in due course, and by March 2020 Relief had successfully chased her son Steve away and had given birth to another male calf that we named Max. I found Steve living in a small channel of the river, but still in relatively close proximity to his family. Relief had inflicted a couple of slashes on his hips to remind him to keep away from the family's pool. As often happens, he had not even met his younger brother, having been chased out before the new calf was born.

Tembia, the other mature bull who lives upstream from us, appears far more tolerant with his family than is usual, perhaps because their pools in the river are larger. With more water to move around in, the juvenile males are not in such close contact with their mothers as they often are in Kuchek's family. Some juvenile males even get to stay with Tembia's family until they are around five years old. Sadly, that was not the case with Kuchek, where not one male has managed to stay in the pod after about two-and-a-half years of age. Perhaps this is because Kuchek is younger and less experienced than Tembia, and it's possible that when he is older, his attitude towards his sons will change.

One evening at the end of May we were sitting in the house when who should arrive on the tiny lawn in front of our house, but young Steve. I recognised him immediately as he still had a cut on his hip from when Relief had chased him away from the family. Blackface, a mature female, had visited us once before, and Surprise, another mature cow, had come along a couple of times. Steve was the first juvenile male hippo to pay us a visit, and he reappeared the following night. He grazed our lawn for about an hour and then moved away. This was only the third time in all of our years of living with the hippos that one of them had appeared and cropped the lawn – what little lawn there was. (Living with animals does take its toll on attempts to grow flowers or a lawn. However, I preferred the company of the animals to a beautiful garden, so I accepted this, and did my best to keep as much lawn as we could. Any flowers were limited to a few hanging baskets, strategically placed out of reach of the ever-inquisitive baboons.)

We have had many animals at our back door over the years, feeding either in daylight or at night. It had all begun with Arthur warthog; then, following him, along came the 'subservient' baboons who were not able to feed with the main troop due to their lower ranking. They arrived at night once word got out that Arthur was getting horse cubes. Later, Arthur brought his female, Jenny, and then their offspring to feed nightly at our back door. Bonny and Clyde, the bush pigs, found us about a year after the warthogs and they, too, became permanent fixtures at the back door, usually arriving after Arthur and his family had left.

Bush pigs are nocturnal feeders, and in the daytime they find a ledge to lie under in a rocky area, or they stay in long grass or under bushes. They are quite different from warthogs, which are diurnal animals and normally remain safely underground at night in holes dug out by antbears, or aardvark as they are known in South Africa. Bush pigs can be a lot more ferocious than warthogs and if they feel threatened they can slash an adversary with their tusks, which are sharp as knives. Bonny and Clyde initially arrived full of fear, and mock-charged at the door when we opened it to put out horse cubes. But they quickly realised that we were on their side and that this hotel had a good daily menu. They made our home a regular stopover on their nightly outings in search of food.

Now it was Steve's turn. Two nights after his first appearance he was back again, but this time he didn't just eat the lawn. As I was to learn, Steve hippo is pretty smart, and when he found all the others at the back door getting stuck into the horse cubes, he joined them. He had eaten horse cubes before in the drought and I'm sure he remembered their smell. He calmly stood right next to all the baboons, which at night could number up to about 20, as well as the two bush pigs, and began munching up the horse cubes. He appeared untroubled by baboons encroaching on his space, sometimes under his stomach, as they ate their cubes, and pigs right near his nose. They all ate amicably around each other.

Initially, Steve was nervous of me when I opened the door to put the food on the ground. He would run away a short distance and then stand and watch what I was doing, but as the evenings passed he became more confident, and would only step back a few paces when the door opened. At that stage he must have weighed in at about 450 kilograms, nearly half a ton, so he was by no means small. He was certainly much bigger than the pigs or the baboons, but he was gentle with them all, just quietly munching away, side by side.

Within a week I could open the door when he was feeding and shine a torch to take photos of him and he didn't move off. In fact, I would talk to him all the time and he, like my hippo Bob, who had died back in 2004, really appeared to enjoy hearing my voice.

I would tell him how handsome and clever he was and continue chatting away while I took photos and videos of him. It was such a wonderful feeling to have a hippo right at the back door; but, more importantly, I was close enough to smell him, see every hair on his body and get within a few metres without fear of him – and he without fear of me.

Although I have lived in close proximity with hippos for nearly 30 years, it was still a source of absolute wonder to be able to interact with Steve like this at the back door, of being only a metre away from a juvenile male hippo. I began posting photos of Steve on social media and within a very short time he began to have his own followers, all enjoying hearing about him and seeing him at such close quarters. By now he was letting me video him without any problems, but he was only like this with me, and was still afraid when Jean-Roger came nearby.

I knew, however, that if this was going to be a regular evening event he would have to get used to Jean, as well as to any volunteers who would be coming here to stay with us. For the next few years Steve came along and with time I managed to introduce him, albeit only at the back door, to our volunteers and some friends. He accepted Jean-Roger but without the same look in his eyes as with me. With all the other people I made sure I was always right next to the door when I opened it to reassure Steve. This allowed them to have the incredible pleasure of safely meeting a wild five-year-old hippo within selfie range without disturbing him.

Then Covid hit and all of our paying volunteers had to cancel their plans. The whole of 2020 passed without one single person visiting us at home, so Steve was my main entertainment and I think he knew I needed a special friend during that period.

Thanks to the close proximity to the hippos that I now enjoyed, I was constantly learning more about them, and also learning to expect the unexpected. In all the time I have lived at Hippo Haven I have walked the same bush paths covering the same terrain again and again, and yet there are never two days on which my experience is exactly the same. There is always something to attract one's attention, and a new experience to be had. It's the same with studying hippo behaviour – I never stop learning from them.

For instance, I thought I had heard most of the calls that hippos make, but Steve taught me another call and he used it regularly once he got to know me. A hippo's purr is somewhat like a cat's but much louder, as befits their size, and with a bit more of a rumble in the tone. They do this to attract attention and whenever Steve pitches up at the back door he will purr to announce his arrival, so that he can get his nightly feed. If I talk to him before opening the door, while looking at him through the mesh gauze that covers the windows, he will purr a lot. It's as if he is saying, 'Hey, come on, where is my dinner?' It's an incredible sound, and one I had never had the privilege of hearing before.

Steve was, by now, often coming within touching distance of me and he wasn't afraid of me at all. As time passed he became more confident in having me right by his side, with the door wide open, and sometimes he would arrive at the house in daylight or at dawn, or often in the late afternoon. I would see him walking from far away in the bush and I would call his name. Just like a dog or a horse, he would lift up his head and start running towards me. I would stand outside and wait for him and, to be honest, it often made me cry, as how many people have a wild hippo who comes at the run when they call him, and appears really happy to see them?

Of course, I would back off a bit when he was getting too close as he is still a hippo, so it would be easy for him to knock me down by accident. I don't think he would, but best not to put it to the test. When I see how calm and relaxed he is with the whole troop of baboons and the bush pigs, some feeding right under his tummy and around his legs, then I think he would probably act exactly that way with me. Our relationship grows stronger with every day that passes. I admit that I have touched his nose and stroked it on quite a few occasions. I just couldn't resist.

I had developed a special relationship with Bob, my favourite bull back in the nineties from more or less the day we arrived, but had never touched him or any other live hippo. Bob would, just like Steve, come along to where I was standing by the riverbed when I called his name. He would stop very close to me but, like all the other hippos, he was in the river and I was not. Often when I called him from the edge of the water he would move underwater at speed, running along the bottom, and this rapidly approaching tidal wave of water would be all I could see. Then up would pop his huge hippo head and often he would then open his mouth in a wide hippo gape – his way of greeting this human friend. With Steve it's different: we are both on land and so the very first time I touched his nose it was a tentative light stroke and then I quickly moved back into the house away from the open door, just in case he took umbrage. I should have known better. He not only seemed to enjoy it, he was telling me in his own hippo way to do it again. So I did.

I still only touch him for a brief second or two on his nose, and often he gapes afterwards, but with soft eyes, without any anger. He loves it – of this I am one hundred percent sure. I only touch him when he is at ease, which I can tell by his eyes, his posture and his ear movements. When his father, Kuchek, is close by and trying to harass him he is much more on his guard. Not with me, but he is very aware of the sounds around him and always keeps his options open so that he can flee if Kuchek suddenly arrives.

So far, Kuchek has never come into the yard when we are awake at night and have the generator on. Luckily, Stevie seems to leave once we turn off the generator; he knows it's our sleep time. Kuchek, however, frequently arrives when we have gone to bed, sprays his dung on any object he finds – the tap, a flowerpot, a bush – and goes on his way. He is advertising that this is his territory, that it has been hard won and will be defended to the death.

There are not many places that young male hippos can move to in safety. Some move to one of the other river systems and are killed by a resident male hippo there, others may be sport-hunted. I cannot stop the hunting of hippos away from the Turgwe River, although I do theoretically have an understanding with the two sport hunting operators near to us, on the other side of the river or downstream. The owners do comply but, tragically, three of the hippos from here have been shot by the employees of one of the operators.

Recently all the people in the Conservancy who hunt have decided not to have hippos on their quota, and they are not even allowed to use them in animal control. Because of the limited number of hippos left in this entire Conservancy, they have realised that it's best to leave them in peace. Even if a hippo is supposedly causing problems and could previously be shot as a 'problem animal', this is no longer legal, which is a huge relief for me.

The death of any animal, be it from natural events or, much worse, human intervention, takes away something inside of me, creating a void, an emptiness, a physical pain. But I tell myself to stay positive, remain optimistic, try to entertain good thoughts and limit those that are negative. It is extremely difficult at times and the worst situations that I have experienced here are mainly due not to animals, but to my fellow human beings: to their attitudes and actions, both past and present.

17

People pressure

I write about animals and the exciting and sometimes amazing experiences of living with them, but while many of the hippo followers think we live in a kind of paradise, there is a downside to this life: people pressure. Most of us know what it's like to be in a situation where our personal values are at variance with someone else's, or when jealousy, bullying and competitiveness are directed at us. Problems here occur because there is little structure, and the 'normality' that prevails is quite different from that in, say, France or the UK, where Jean-Roger and I were born, respectively. Our lives here can be fraught with danger, fear, mistrust and worry, all of which come not from the wilderness and life in the wild, but from human beings.

In over three decades it has always been people who have disrupted, and sometimes nearly destroyed our equilibrium, our health or, at times, even our lives. Politics in Europe or the United States has many downsides, but in those relatively functioning democracies one has certain inalienable rights, including the right to be outspoken. This is seldom the case in third-world countries, and has not been the story here in Zimbabwe since 2000. Neither of us is involved with politics. We do not vote, and we keep away from all the disputes and political posturing that occur in election years.

Corruption happens everywhere but, in first-world countries, people are concerned about it. Here in Zimbabwe, corruption seems to be entrenched in the conduct of practically everyone in a position of power, in one way or another. It is an altogether authoritarian system and the people have to do as they are told. And when there is not a fully functioning system of justice, anything can happen. So every now and then people use force. This might be verbal threatening or, worse, physical violence towards others to get what they want. We and our neighbours have had this happen to us and have first-hand knowledge of how intimidating a large mob of people can be.

Our experience has been that, in Zimbabwe, issues are seldom discussed in a one-on-one conversation. Rather, among local people, stating one's case requires the backing of a crowd – as many hangers-on as can be fitted into a lorry, or even a bus or, if necessary, on foot. It is crowd intimidation at its best. Having a mob of some 20 noisy, angry men arrive in a vehicle and drive into your property as if it's their own is not fun. They don't wait at the entrance to announce their presence. They pile out of their vehicle and, if you are not quick enough to meet them, they start wandering around your yard or garden as if it's their own home. No friendly faces, no polite 'How are you?' – just intimidation in numbers. Then when you, the proprietor, arrive to meet them with a scowl on your face, demanding in a not-too-pleasant manner who they are and what they are doing on your property, they accuse you of being the bad guy. And, being a woman, I automatically fail to qualify for any rights at all, let alone challenging the mob.

In spite of the extreme discomfort these incidents cause, I have no choice but to stand up for my home, for the staff and our animals. These invasions don't happen as much now as they did in the 2000s, but they can still occur at any time. Bullying in this part of the world is massive, especially towards women.

We have learnt that a group of men walking in the bush is usually up to no good. Here in the Conservancy the bush is not for walkers, it is the animals' habitat. Plus, this area comprising the Conservancy and related communities is a high-protection zone for the rhino, which means no-one is supposed to be wandering around. So when, occasionally, I am on my regular morning run or out in the bush to view the hippos and I come into contact with men who are not supposed to be in the area, and who are often the very ones we have arrested before for poaching, it's heart-stopping. When you are a few kilometres from your home and there are no neighbours, no shops to run to, just bush and animals, you have to stand up for yourself. I try to remain strong and not let them see my fear, and so you become outwardly a lion, but a weak kitten deep inside.

Sport hunters in the past used to hunt in our area, but once the land got taken over by the land invaders they could no longer come here to shoot. To be honest, in some ways we prefer having the new settlers (as they are now called) living around us: they are not too close by, and mostly don't poach. They live on handouts and anything they can grow on this land, which, as it is drought prone, is suitable mainly for wildlife.

The invaders, who were more or less told by the government to come here, all have other homes in the communities that they left in order to seize settled property. Their own land and their homes are looked after by one of their women – it is common for Zimbabwean men to have several wives. The invaders came here in the early 2000s when they were told they could take the land, poach and do whatever they wanted to the people who owned the title deeds for that land. Initially it was a free-for-all of poaching, with absolutely no law and order, or any controls – but that was then. Now, some 20 years later, a semblance of law and order has returned and 90 percent of the same people live quietly, not poaching or threatening their neighbours. However, there are always those who love to break rules, who steal, kill animals and do whatever takes their fancy. They are always the same men from the same families.

In our area there are four families like that, and further away from us, where Tembia and his hippos live, there is a village about five kilometres inland where there are at least six or seven families with a tradition of thieving. Over the last two decades, either our rangers or those from Humani – a much larger force – have caught the same guys regularly. Then, having caught the intruders, the whole palaver of getting them to the police, then going to court over and over again, is not only time-consuming, it's also very expensive.

The police station is a 90-minute drive away on bad roads, and the court is two hours away. Courts in this area are not like those you see on TV! They have no aircon, so the prosecutors and magistrates all sit fanning themselves with pieces of paper. The courts smell of people's sweat and fear; they are not pleasant places. You can spend

125

an entire day in court from 9 a.m. to 5 p.m., and even then you are not guaranteed that the person you want prosecuted will be seen on that day; you may be required to attend repeatedly in the hope of getting a conviction, sometimes over a period of up to four months. And what happens frequently is that the suspect eventually gets a light sentence, or community service; but nine times out of ten they get a paltry fine, which is far less than the so-called value of the animal that they have killed. Or they are even let off entirely.

Yet, if you don't follow up on a poacher or criminal by going to court, his family or friends or high-up connections will go along and exert pressure on the magistrate to release the suspect. He may then run off for a year or so, but on his return he could start up all over again and be back poaching the very next day. Then the whole rigmarole starts up all over again. However, you cannot give in, asking 'what is the point?' You cannot allow the financial strain on the charity you run or the wear and tear on your vehicles to defeat you.

All the animals that the poachers kill are for commercial sale. These are not poor, starving people trying to feed their families, as there is a lot of aid coming into Africa – handouts are a regular occurrence. Money is all that matters to them, and poaching wildlife is a very lucrative business.

Most sport hunters are from overseas, the majority of them American, and they come to Africa to shoot trophies. Their dollars buy them a safari camp, sometimes for up to a month, for themselves and a couple of fellow hunters or their wives or mistresses. It gives them time away from their high-pressure jobs, as they are often lawyers or top-end business executives, even doctors and occasionally vets! Some come to hunt specific animals like an elephant, buffalo, lion or giraffe. Their goal is to bag that particular animal, but they may still shoot other animals in between, should the opportunity arise.

I have met many of these hunters and have noticed some common characteristics among them: a need to control, to dominate, to be praised often and to have people fawning over their prowess. They are often elderly, their body is not what it used to be, and they think hunting enhances their manliness and prestige in the eyes of others.

Some who have major health issues have been known to shoot illegally from cars. And even hunters who are able to walk may resist setting off on their own two feet and walking all day long in the dust, dirt and often extreme heat. Such men take the easy route to success, and are able to tip the professional hunters, trackers, skinners and the whole menagerie of people involved to ensure they get to kill the animal they are after, in order to hang it on their wall, or display it in a huge trophy room in their mansion back in the United States. Of course, money talks!

Ethics in the hunting world does exist, but money will always tempt those who are prepared to turn a blind eye and, sadly, in three decades we have often witnessed unethical behaviour. One trick is to lure cats such as leopards or lions from one area, which is non-hunting, to a hunting area by dragging the carcass of a dead animal out of the safe zone to a place just across the boundary, allowing the scent of the meat to attract the predators across the border – a ploy that was used in this country to shoot the famous lion, Cecil. Another is getting information from informers about radio-collared animals like elephants. The minute that animal steps out of a protected zone the hunter is already there waiting to kill it, even if it is only metres away from safety.

It is obviously not just in hunting where ethics are ignored by some. Such behaviour is widespread, but when it's an animal that pays the price it turns me into a very angry person. I have learnt, though, that anger directed at these people, who are often inwardly angrier than I am, never really pays. I have tried education and taking hunters to meet the hippos, but the majority of them insist on having a weapon with them and are often very afraid. It's clear that they continue to view wildlife both as a threat – and as fair game.

One such example involved a white Zimbabwean who used to be a schoolteacher and is an apparently pleasant, articulate, interesting and polite man. However, he is now a professional hunter, taking sport hunters to kill animals, which in no way accords with my own feelings. Whenever he is hunting on a property to the south of us he pops in with his clients to see me and to show the hunters my relationship with the hippos.

Like all the Zimbabwean professional hunters in this area, he is very aware of my opposition to hunting but, unusually, he actually listens to my opinions. Whenever I try to explain my views to the other hunters, most of them shoot me down in flames or criticise me, or call me a bunny hugger. I still try, as I think it's important to have these discussions and to hear different viewpoints.

The following incident took place in 2019 when I was feeding animals during the drought. This hunter pitched up in his vehicle with two burly, big-bellied South African hunters. One immediately got out of the vehicle with the Zimbabwe hunter, but the other one quickly shut his window, remaining inside the vehicle. I asked what the problem was and the other South African explained that his mate was very afraid of vervet monkeys.

Now, as many will know, a vervet is about the size of a large pussycat, but okay, lots of people have phobias. Our baboons were not even at the house then and I wondered what he would do, locked in the car, if they appeared, with some of the males nearly as tall as me when standing on their hind legs!

The plan was to take the three of them (although the hunter in the car refused to budge, and was left behind) down to the feeding station and leave them on a large rocky area above the food station so they would be out of sight of the hippos but able to see them feed. Then I would continue down to the feeding place and, with Silas helping me, lay out the hay and food for the hippos. I felt that at least they would get to see that hippos are not spontaneously vicious, as many people claim, and hoped that this visual education might in a tiny way enlighten them.

I knew that Kuchek, if he came along, would give them a fantastic show. Sure enough, he arrived with his females and youngsters. They waited at a distance and as I finished putting out the food I spoke to Kuchek, as I always do, saying, 'Okay, boy, you can come now'. And, as always, he began walking eagerly towards the food while Silas and I slowly backed away. Only a metre or two separated us from the hippos. When I climbed up to the rock again I could see that the

South African hunter was wide-eyed with astonishment and, despite his being quite safe from the hippos, his hands were shaking.

When it started getting dark I said it was time to leave and asked them to get up slowly from their seated positions and crouch down a little so that they did not attract the hippos' attention as we walked back up to the house. Well, what happened next amazed me. The South African man hit the floor and belly-crawled off the rock, before doing a wonderful impersonation of a hugely hump-backed figure, which he maintained practically all the way back to the house. To say he was afraid was an understatement. The professional hunter just gave me a kind of crooked smile of embarrassment, but the two men were his clients and so he had to be polite. The other man finally got out of the car and into the 'safety' of the house, where his friend, now full of himself, told me how he and his mate had stalked and killed a buffalo only the day before. Like hell, I thought!

If I lived in the first world I would join protests and be a voice for animals. Here in Africa the only way you can protest – that is, if you wish to remain in one piece mentally and physically – is by example. In my case, even 30 years down the road, it often doesn't work.

A landowner who has a hunting safari setup on the other side of the Turgwe River will never accept what I do here, even though we protect what was once his land before the invasions, a part that lies on our side of the river. We have done this since 2001, through years of physical threats from the people snaring and killing the wildlife, and from politically connected people; and even now there is still harassment towards us, although it's much less intense than it was in the bad years. We don't protect the land for the landowner, we do it for the hippos and all the other animals that live in the area.

For two decades we and our rangers have patrolled that piece of land, removing snares, catching poachers and doing all we can to save the resident animals. Our rangers go there as much as four or five times a week and they have no weapons, only sticks. I visit the hippos up there – the family of Tembia, Bob's son – as often as I can. Either we walk or drive up to them, but it is we who maintain the only dirt road to the hippos. We have had our lives threatened by the people who invaded, and yet we have never stopped our vigilance.

Every year when the reeds that grow close to the hippos' pools in the river get too thick, we cut a passage for access and better visibility. Buffalos, elephants, lions, even a hippo could so easily be tucked up in the reeds, making it quite dangerous to walk in there. If you corner an animal, however inadvertently, then it will go for you.

The owner of the land on the opposite bank built a safari camp there, mainly for his photographic tourists, not his hunters, who stay at a camp downstream from us on the other side of the Turgwe. Recently we sent our rangers to cut the reeds so that I could approach the hippos and count, photograph and video them. Most of this is done not for me, but for the adoption process, in which I send people regular photos and videos as part of the adoption package. Financially, this comes back to the Turgwe Hippo Trust as a benefit for the hippos and other animals, and helps run the THT on a monthly basis.

When we cut a swathe through the reeds this time we got a very angry Whatsapp message from the landowner opposite, saying, 'How dare you open up the reeds there? It's directly opposite our safari camp and people paying to stay there do not want to see other people'.

This I understand. We don't go there daily and never spend more than an hour or so; and they don't have clients every day. As soon as I have recorded as much as I can of the hippos there, I back out. I may take the odd volunteer up there when the rangers let us know that nobody is in camp, but at all times we respect the safari camp on the other bank. It is still a dangerous area to walk into, but at least with the opening of a passageway we can see if a buffalo or an elephant is approaching, or is in the thicker parts that we haven't slashed.

But the lodge owner was furious. He said, 'What the hell does Karen need photos of the hippos for? Hasn't she got enough? She must have taken thousands over the years.'

So even now, after 30 years of living and working to protect the hippos and other wildlife, removing snares and employing rangers to catch poachers, in his eyes all I am doing is taking photographs. There remains little understanding of the enormous amount of conservation work we have done in the area over the years, but our commitment is nevertheless unwavering.

Some of the baby warthogs who come with their mothers to the area around our homestead.

The rescued Three-banded courser, Valentine, was eventually returned to the wild. She visited us later on to show that she was alive and well.

Lizzie, a Lizard buzzard, is another of our rescue birds. We hand-reared her and released her back to the wild when she was able to hunt and fend for herself.

When the Turgwe River is in flood, the causeway is sometimes not crossable for up to a month, sometimes even longer.

In normal years when the rains arrive, the river briefly turns into a raging torrent. This view is just below our house and the headquarters of the Turgwe Hippo Trust.

A very special hippo, Steve first came to our house in 2020, shortly after his mother had driven him away from his family in anticipation of the birth of her new calf. Here he opens his mouth to give a large gape.

Steve meets the warthogs Sally and her offspring Ben — this was the first encounter between these two species at Hippo Haven.

Bob, the hippo that prompted my study of the behaviour of these magnificent animals. Bob was also the catalyst for our starting a not-for-profit organisation for the long-term survival of the Turgwe hippos and registering the Turgwe Hippo Trust.

Bob was so relaxed in my presence that he had no qualms about mating with his females right in front of me.

Blackface had been mistreated by humans, an experience she never forgot, and so she could be cantankerous at times. She often mock charged me, keeping me from becoming too blasé around the hippos. In all the years I have lived with hippos, Blackface was the only one to remain angry and afraid.

Me on one of my frequent visits to see the hippos in the river.

The son of Bob and Lace, Tembia was conceived in the devastating drought of 1992.
It was during that drought that I sourced food for the hippos for the first time.

Tembia became one of two dominant bulls in 2006 when he was only 13 years old. He had very
recognisable white markings on his toes and inner front legs.

Tembia, in his prime, showing off his splendour. Taken in August 2022, this photograph is the last one I took of him.

Jean-Roger and Friendly the baboon relax in the gazebo. Friendly and the other baboons that regularly arrive at our home are not hand-reared; they are all completely wild.

Looking down towards the Turgwe River, I am surrounded by wild baboons and a few cats: Lucky and Pretty just behind me and Nelson, one of our rescue cats, perched on my shoulder. All the wildlife and our domestic cats get on together.

18

Wounds and self healing

The first warthog ever to arrive at our house was Arthur, and I am convinced that the warthogs that have come along since his days in the 1990s are all in some way related to him. It is too much of a coincidence to imagine that a succession of warthogs would begin finding their way to our home without word having been passed along. But related or otherwise, individual warthogs have strong characters and some have been involved in incidents that make me remember them more than others. Perky is a good example.

He was born to Winny, and when he had grown into a fully mature male he disappeared for some time. It's not unusual for males to move away: they prefer to live alone or with other males, while the females tend to stay with their immediate relations: young offspring, mothers, sisters and aunts. Males come back to their sounders when the females are ready to be mated; and they return to our house if they are hungry, remembering that it's a pretty reasonable stop-off place. But otherwise they are out and about, living their warthog lives. So when Perky did not come back I was not particularly worried; many a male had followed the same pattern of behaviour, sometimes returning even after a year or so away.

One morning Silas called me saying that a male had come in with a wounded foot. It turned out to be Perky, and the wound was serious. Practically his entire back right foot was hanging from just a thin sinew. He could walk, but was having to put pressure on the actual foot and this must have been causing him excruciating pain.

It would be so easy for the foot to get caught in a branch or rock, as he had no control over the part that was hanging loose.

Perky had always been a friendly male. Even so, the males have very large tusks and even if they accept us humans into their lives, we still have to be extremely careful. Human skin is by no means as tough as their hide; just a gentle nudge from a lower canine can slice human skin open. Jean had discovered this early on and learnt a valuable lesson. He had been carrying a bucket full of horse cubes to feed to the warthogs and Sally, one of the larger females, decided he was walking a little too slowly. She gave him a gentle nudge and her lower canine cut into his flesh, leaving an open wound on his calf about three centimetres long and quite deep. It was pointless driving for three hours on bad roads just to have a stitch or two to close the wound, so Jean left it to heal itself, and it thankfully healed well. We did use aloe vera, which is one plant we have managed to grow and keep the baboons from pulling up. And we always have on hand essential lavender and tea tree oils, which work amazingly well on cuts, stings and wounds.

Although Perky had huge lower canines, he had a very calm nature and had never been overly excitable towards any of us. I decided there was only one thing we could do to help, which was to cut into the hanging sinew so that the hoof and foot would fall away and leave a stump, with nothing left that could get caught and cause him further pain. The sinew was dry and stringy, so it was not as if cutting it away would hurt him. But would he allow me to do it? I gave him some food on his own and asked Jean to distract him by scratching behind his ears, which warthogs simply adore. Taking the garden secateurs, I stationed myself by his hind legs. Then I got Jean to scratch Perky's belly, hoping that he would lie on his side, as no self-respecting warthog will walk away from a belly rub; it's pure bliss for them.

Perky did exactly what I wanted him to do: he lay down and turned onto his side, fortunately with the bad foot nearest to me. In a matter of seconds I had cut the sinew, and the bottom part of his hoof and the foot fell off. Although he now had one leg a bit shorter than the others, he could at least move around on his other three legs, and with surprising dexterity. And he would no longer be in extreme pain.

Within a month he was putting weight on the stump, and he could run and move around in the bush with amazing agility. With only a little intervention from us, the power of Nature had healed her own.

We had seen the same with baboons coming along to the house with devastating injuries, be it an arm practically hanging off, or their faces ripped by a fight and sometimes even a jawline punctured by teeth jutting through from inside. These injuries often resulted from males fighting each other. Yet, within a matter of weeks you would never know they had been hurt, with perhaps a tiny scar being all that remained. I think that primates' high Vitamin C levels – thanks to the amount of wild fruit they consume – enables them to heal particularly well.

Our immune systems are remarkably efficient at healing sometimes near-catastrophic wounds and, in the wild, animals are entirely dependent on their body's curative powers. The ability of wildlife to recover from injuries is further enhanced by their natural, unadulterated diet, as long as there are no detrimental circumstances such as a severe drought.

I have also seen hippos heal after being severely injured. As Steve hippo grew, he became a threat to his father, Kuchek. Steve was far too young to even think of taking over a family but, in Kuchek's view, any male was a threat as it could later become competition for him, for his territory and even for his own family. So while sons are chased away from their families, often by their own mother when she is about to give birth again, it's always the dominant bull of the family who is the enforcer, making sure that no young male, once evicted, even tries to come home again.

Some young male hippos don't make it through this stage of their development. With their advantage in weight and experience, dominant bulls can kill them, even if not intentionally. In the years that I have worked for these hippos, eight males have been killed by their own father or an unrelated bull, or even, occasionally, by a cow who has a male calf and won't allow an older male sibling near her and her baby.

Steve had been coming to the house for a couple of years when, one day, Kuchek attacked him. Kuchek must have come across Steve down in the riverbed, which is part of the dominant bull's territory. I was awoken at four in the morning to the sound of loud running feet. Although it was still dark, through our mesh windows I could see a huge shape rushing past our bedroom, followed by an even bigger shape. I realised immediately that Steve was being chased by an enraged Kuchek.

Jean, as always, could sleep through anything, so I grabbed the torch and started screaming at Kuchek, 'Leave Stevie alone!' I ran from the bedroom to the living area, shining my torch outside and constantly shouting at Kuchek. I heard the fence being bashed as Steve was trapped against it by Kuchek. He had missed the exit where the gates are always left open for him to come in and graze our small lawn at night. Steve was obviously in a total panic now that Kuchek had caught up with him.

I kept on shouting, and ran to the back door to confront Kuchek. I realised that this was kind of foolish as Kuchy weighs in at about two tons, but he was hurting my boy Steve, and that was not allowed. Our home was supposed to be a safe haven for all. As I dashed outside, Kuchek shot past at speed and I saw that Steve was quite a way in front of him. They rushed down the bank to the river. I couldn't follow them in the dark, so instead I ran to the front of the house and from the top of the riverbank I continued screaming at Kuchek to leave Steve alone. I heard both of them thundering through the water and then it went quiet.

At dawn we tracked the night's events and, to my dismay, I found quite a lot of blood against the fence where Kuchek had caught up with Steve. There were drops of blood leading from there and covering rocks down to the river, and more blood on the sandy beach at the water's edge. Although there was a lot of blood, at least it wasn't arterial, so Steve wouldn't die from loss of blood. I found where he had entered the river; he had, by then, managed to get away from Kuchek, whose tracks were no longer imprinted in the sand.

I was beside myself with fear for Steve. But these are wild animals, and all I could do was wait and hope that Steve was not mortally wounded, and that he would at some stage return to the house. The longest he had stayed away was around 10 days but when after 30 days he had not returned I was really worried. Then the rangers found his fresh tracks. I went with them and, sure enough, they matched Steve's size of footprint. And they were quite near to the house. It had to be him!

On the 32nd day Steve arrived at the house. Not only was I ecstatic to see him, but he could not have picked a better moment to come home. I was in deep pain and grief as our darling mongoose Squiggle had died the previous morning. Steve knew, and he came back for me. I absolutely believe that Squiggle sent him to me.

He had a horrendous hole in his hip area, about 10 to 15 centimetres in diameter, and it was quite deep. It was clear that Kuchek had ripped out a big chunk of Steve's flesh using his huge canines or incisors. But at least the wound was dry and clean, and not obviously causing him pain or other problems. Steve was a little nervous; not of me, but rather just generally wary, and keeping a close eye on his surroundings. I assume this was the first real lesson he'd had on how a dominant bull (in this instance, his father) could behave towards him, and he had got off relatively lightly. Amazingly, within one month Steve's wound had closed up as if it had been stitched and, although it left an impressive scar, it healed well.

Another incident that happened at home involved the two bush pigs that used to come along each evening for their nightly snack, and a leopard. Both pigs are adults, but I think Bonny is much older and could possibly be Clyde's mother. Bush pigs are supposed be very aggressive and dangerous. Not so with Bonny or Clyde: within days of their first arriving, Bonny was allowing both Jean and me to open the back door and put the food down in front of her. She just stood there without any fear and with a gentle expression in her eyes. Jean could even scratch the side of her face. Clyde was much more nervous, but never aggressive. So they became regular visitors at night, feeding alongside the subservient troop of baboons (who arrived when the main troop had gone off to roost in the trees) and Steve the hippo – all of them eating contentedly at the back door.

One night there were just the two bush pigs at the door (the baboons had gone off to bed in the trees, and Steve had not come that night), and I had thrown them some horse cubes. We were thinking about turning off our generator and going to bed when I heard the most terrible squealing. It sounded like a human scream, but continuous and blood-curdling. I rushed to the door, but could see nothing in the dark. I got my torch and realised that the screams were coming from under the nearby bougainvillea bush. I still couldn't see who was screaming, but there was no sign of either Bonny or Clyde. Then I noticed a brown body tucked deep under the bush; it was Bonny, and she was doing all the screaming. She didn't appear to be hurt – she was just making the most fearsome noise. And then I heard a low growl. At first I thought it was a lion. Whatever it was, it was on the other side of the bush and trying to get at Bonny. There was only one thing to do and that was to frighten whatever it was to make it leave Bonny alone.

I had made a vow to myself that we would protect, to the best of our ability, any wild animal that came to our home, the back yard and garden; not just against people hunting them but from any situation where a human could step in and help them. This was the line I drew. Out in the bush I could not intervene with animals, but at home I could, and I would.

By now Jean had joined me at the back door and was telling me in no uncertain terms to stay there and not think about moving towards the bushes. He knows me well. Around the back door is a layer of small stones to keep the dust down, as the animals dig up any grass I have tried to plant there. I started picking up stones and hurling them at the bush, avoiding Bonny. I knew that my little stones couldn't hurt whatever was threatening the bush pig, but I might be able to scare the predator off. I continued to chuck handfuls of stones and, after a couple of minutes of this onslaught, we heard a really loud growl-grunt. Jean shone his torch in that direction and the animal moved off at speed. It was a very large leopard.

Bonny initially stayed put under her bush; and after perhaps half an hour, when she was certain the leopard had moved off, she emerged and proceeded to eat the horse cubes as if nothing at all had happened. Clyde must have decided to skip supper that night!

136

Then, at some point, this pair of bush pigs stopped coming to our door at night and we have never seen them again

One night about a year after this event five new bush pigs arrived at the house and have continued coming every night ever since. Eventually the new bush pigs produced four piglets and then we had nine pigs coming to the back door.

Then just recently another incident occurred. We were actually awake, reading, when we heard an almighty crash. I shot up, running into the kitchen and found the heavy duty glass from the bottom of the back door completely caved in. The bush pigs were all screaming just as Bonny had done when she was attacked. I rushed out and in the moonlight I saw a lioness holding one of the babies. I shouted and screamed at her and even ran towards her. To my utter astonishment she dropped the baby and ran off grunting and growling. Jean appeared with a torch and we approached the baby. It was lying on its side kicking its legs but it couldn't get up. There was a wound on the top of its short stumpy neck but there wasn't much blood.

The lioness had moved off as had all the other pigs but the baby was struggling. I wasn't sure if this was from shock or if it was internally damaged but I felt we had to give it a chance to recover, as wild animals are exceedingly tough. I stayed with the piggy while Jean woke up the rangers to help bring across the heavy Land Rover canopy. We had dismantled this ages before and it was now unused. I wanted to put the pig in something strong enough so that if the lioness came back she could not get it. Safely under the canopy, the little pig was still thrashing around a bit and obviously not in a good way. Still, I felt we had to try, so we left it and all of us went to our respective beds. I was up and out with the dawn next morning but the piggy was no better; it was paralysed and unable to stand up. There was only one solution, one that we both hated: Jean-Roger had to shoot her. We have a shotgun in case of rabid dogs, and in this case it put the poor little animal out of her misery.

The pigs didn't return for six weeks but then, one night, they were back and thankfully have been coming to our back door ever since.

19

Squiggle

How to express loss? We have all experienced it and when it's an animal that cannot talk to you of their pain or sickness, and the animal dies, you find yourself condemning every move you made. The loss is too hard to bear.

Squiggle was my (or should I say, our) baby, our child. Both of us felt such love for her, much stronger than any love either of us had ever experienced. Although Jean was never really an 'animal person', being with me for all these years has changed him. He admits to not feeling the depth of love or dedication to animals that I do; nor does he feel the freedom of spirit that I receive from them. But he understands how it is for me, and over the years animals have become important to him too.

People tend to think that animal-loving women like me who don't have children automatically love and relate to animals as if they were children. This had never been the case until Squiggle came along. Jean-Roger and I hand-reared her together, from the day we found her lost in the bush all those years ago, with her umbilical cord still attached, and with only one eye open. We fed her every two hours, day and night, for three weeks, which is very condensed in relation to a human child's needs, but was exhausting at the time. She was so little, weighing only 50 grams, and yet her tenacity of spirit and sheer determination to survive, plus the love we both gave her, pulled her through, and so she survived. We tended to her every need as devotedly as any parents, and for nine years and two months she was our child. We found our lives revolving around her.

I have experienced similar bonds with a pony, a cat, a dog and with two hippos, Bob and Steve. Yet our relationship with Squiggle went deeper. She slept with us nightly, lived with us and was very much part of our home. We would never go away and leave her at home for more than three nights; and most of the time, if possible, she travelled with us. She loved being in her small travelling cage, on the road to wherever we were headed. She stayed in various homes in Harare where colleagues and friends allowed her to do so, and she was smuggled into the odd hotel. When we travelled we had to pack more belongings for her than for us, including her three different cages for different situations, her comfort blanket and her snacks.

When we couldn't take her with us on a short trip and absolutely had to leave her at home, she had a cage big enough to house a pony. She stayed in that cage in the living room, with Silas sleeping in the same room to keep an eye on her, although she didn't allow him to handle her. If we ever left home for work or holiday for longer than three days we had to have a house sitter so that Squiggle would be safe. My wonderful friend Mirinda Thorpe from Australia would fly all the way to Zimbabwe to look after our home, the work and the staff but, most importantly, Squiggle. Once, when Mirinda was staying with us, I thought I had lost Squiggle – that she had got out of the house and been hurt. From my reaction then, Mirinda will know what I feel right now.

Squiggle lived in our home with us always. At first, when she was very young, I would take her for outings in the bush, with her sitting on one of my feet as I walked; but as she grew and started venturing into holes and up trees I became paranoid about her safety, and so she lived indoors. Not caged, but in a whole house with a large en suite outside cage, for she had to have sun and grass as well.

Yet she preferred to be indoors with us, either on my shoulder or playing with Jean-Roger. She so loved to play with him! She and Jean had a special play bond and he loved her. She reserved the love-and-cuddle bond mostly for me. She was such a diva and could bite harder than a bull terrier when she wanted to make a point.

As parents do, we indulged her. She was given anything she wanted if we had it to give. She had to have her scrambled eggs cooked to her liking, not to ours. And I sometimes took her breakfast in bed if the weather was particularly cold!

She was shy of strangers but, once she got used to our volunteers, many of them had the pleasure of having Squiggle on their lap or running across their feet. Most of the time she was either playing or sleeping. She also talked a lot through the gauze windows to the cats on the outside of the house. She grew up with our 'inside' cats but, as they died from old age, I didn't allow the 'outside' cats in, as I was afraid they might hurt her – or she them. She was known to have chased baboons out of the house when they occasionally got inside. Five hundred grams of fury up against 40 kilograms with big teeth – no problem at all for Squiggle!

Our mongoose really was everything to us, and her zest for life made her sudden death all the harder to bear: one minute she was okay, and then she was not. My closest friend in Zimbabwe who runs her own animal sanctuary up near Harare, Sarah Carter, asked her vet husband what it was that took our Squiggle. Vinay believes she died from kidney failure. He said that such a tiny mammal would not hang on for long with a kidney problem; and she had passed away so quickly.

At this time my hippo Steve had been absent for many weeks, causing me great concern and anxiety. But my grief and physical pain at the loss of Squiggle was practically unbearable. I had never known body pain as severe as it was then. In my years of loving animals I have had many pass over the rainbow bridge, and in every loss the sorrow, grief and guilt have enveloped me. Yet the loss of Squiggle was a loss like no other. I couldn't physically let her go, and held her from 5 a.m., when she died, for many hours. I couldn't face anyone or anything; I wanted to run and just keep running and never have to face anything ever again. Of course, I couldn't do this – I was running a charity for hippos. I had donating guests arriving that weekend. I had six cats to look after in their respective cottages, along with warthogs, baboons, vervets and bush pigs, which all relied on me and our home for their safety and wellbeing.

We decided to bring two of the cats, Nelson, with one blind eye, and his very old grandmother, Tinkerbell, into the house that day, after we had buried our baby. I didn't think I was being disloyal to

Squiggle, but neither of us could stand the emptiness of the house without her. Also, the two cats had issues, so we thought they would be happy to have a house to live in.

Squiggle gave me more than any living being has ever done, human or animal. I feel half the person I was before she left us, and her loss has closed a part of me that does not seem able to reopen.

This was written with my love, my admiration, my tears and my memories, knowing that Squiggle and I will meet again.

20

Tembia hippo

Having lived and worked with wildlife for so many years, I have reaped many rewards, but there is always underlying concern for the wellbeing of those animals with which I have most closely bonded, and that I have come to love. Domestic animals become accustomed to living with people in their homes, whilst wild animals, of course, have habits of their own and go where they want to go. But I feel deep anxiety when familiar animals simply disappear.

From a young age, hippo bulls are aware that they are different, and it's natural for them to disperse. They are sometimes driven away by their own mother, although it's the dominant bull (usually their father) that ensures the young males stay away – they are, after all, potential challengers for his position. If a cow is pregnant, she may regard her existing male offspring to be a threat to a new calf, particularly if it should turn out to be another male. I have witnessed generations of young bulls having to leave their families.

However, lack of sufficient habitat means that many of these outcast bulls may never reach a stage where they can have their own territory and become the dominant bull in a hippo family. In larger river systems bulls can often live together in bachelor pods with their own familiar territory. But this isn't always possible in small river systems like the Turgwe, where hippo-friendly habitat is in short supply. A lot of the natural habitat of hippos was taken over by land invaders in the early 2000s, even though this area had already been designated a wildlife Conservancy.

The hippo called Bob was my inspiration back in the early nineties. He taught me more about hippos than any text book could, or the experience that I had gained as a safari guide. His image became the logo for the Trust, inspiring me to have the Turgwe Hippo Trust officially gazetted in order to continue as a not-for-profit organisation. I knew this would enable me to do my best for all the hippos.

Tembia was born in 1993. He was the son of Bob, the dominant bull in his family group, and Lace, and he was conceived during that first devastating drought. I was there on 16th June, the day Tembia was born. The realisation that Lace had managed to conceive in those appalling conditions, thanks to my feeding program, was just wonderful. It was a time that changed my life, and that of my husband, forever: it sealed my commitment to the hippos and we both realised we wanted to stay in the bush and live our lives here, continuing to help the hippos.

I named the hippo calf Tembia (not yet knowing his gender) after a Hereford cow that I had raised when I was much younger. She had been found alongside her mother who had a prolapsed uterus and, although the farmer had tried to save her, he was unable to do so. But the calf, amazingly, lived. I named her Tembia and raised her – the first of many cattle that I looked after back then, before I met Jean-Roger. Now it felt appropriate to name the baby hippo after her: it was going to be a special hippo, the first one born out of the 1992 drought – a tragedy that saw the death of thousands of wild animals. Given the status of Bob in my life, it stood to reason that Tembia (who turned out to be a male) would become just as important to me.

Tembia grew over the years into a large, handsome hippo, just like his father. He even had exactly the same markings as Bob on the inside of his mouth – a black streak on the lower jaw. And he had remarkably clear identification marks on his body: white pigmentation behind both his front feet and, later, a rip in his left ear.

Tembia was exceptionally lucky in that he had managed to stay alongside his mother, in his father's family, until he reached five years of age. And then things changed, and Bob wanted him gone. Occasionally the female will intervene on behalf of her calf if she is not already pregnant. In Lace's case, she not only at first stood up to Bob and received quite a few cuts on her body while protecting her son, but she was still determined to keep Tembia with her.

In due course, instead of Tembia's being ousted and having to fend for himself alone, as is the normal rite of passage, Lace left Bob's family and moved with her son some 20 kilometres downstream. There they remained for several years, just the two of them. Then another bull, Robin, found them. Once again, Tembia was lucky: instead of attacking and evicting the young hippo, Robin allowed him to stay. The family continued living in a small pool but, as time passed, Lace became pregnant by Robin. At this point young Tembia was finally chased away. He returned to our area and for a couple more years he lived alone, as so many males have to. At least he had enjoyed the protection and company of his mother for an unusually extended period.

Mature hippo bulls seem to know when another bull dies, even without having knowledge of that bull's territory. Sometimes within a day or so of a bull's death, a new bull will come along from many kilometres away and take on the newly leaderless family at that pool. I have seen this happen on three or four occasions so I don't think it's coincidental.

When Happy, the dominant bull in our area, died, Robin made his way upstream to fill the gap. Lace didn't join him, but remained behind with her new son. By now Tembia was 11 years of age and so he challenged Robin. I happened to be in the area when the fight began. This is the only hippo fight I have witnessed, and watching two bulls attacking one another is not a pleasant experience. I knew I couldn't interfere, as it was natural for a younger bull to challenge an older one for his territory. But I hoped that it wouldn't turn into a fight to the death, which can happen with hippo bulls, depending on the strength of determination on both sides. As the battle raged I did, however, record the action on camera and video.

Although Tembia was much younger and smaller, he was more agile. Robin had an age and weight advantage over his opponent, and years of experience, although his deformed foot made it harder for him to stand square when the two clashed, mouths agape. He wisely headed into the pool, where their fight continued. Robin and Tembia fought on and off in the pool for the entire day. They would open their mouths wide, but without the soft eyes that relaxed hippos show, and then they would push and push at each other in an ongoing contest of strength. Eventually Robin would lunge up out of the water, pitting his entire upper body against Tembia's extended mouth and, if he was able, he would slash at Tembia with his massive lower incisors.

As the day progressed both were bleeding, mainly from head and neck wounds, but neither of them was backing down and this, for me, was very worrying. I feared that Tembia could ultimately lose against Robin's maturity and strength. Then, around late afternoon I witnessed Tembia standing down: his body language made it obvious he no longer wanted to challenge Robin, and he turned tail and moved off. Robin pressed home his advantage by chasing after Tembia and giving him a couple more cuts on his bottom; but by this time Robin was exhausted, and I think it was this that probably saved Tembia's life.

Tembia moved away from the channel of the river he had been living in and I found him up near his father Bob's pool. The next day, information arrived that a dead hippo bull had been found in that area. I rushed up there, my heart in my mouth, fearing I would find Tembia dead; and instead I found my boy Bob. He was in a sitting position with his head resting on a rock in a tiny pool near to his home turf. He had sustained just one severe wound, obviously inflicted by another hippo, not a human. It was right next to his main neck artery, and Bob had bled to death. I was devastated at the loss of this, my first hippo love.

Three days later I was back at Bob's pool and from a distance I noticed a bull in the pool with the females. To my astonishment I found that it was Tembia. Had he killed his father? I will never know, but it just made sense that he probably had. From that day in 2004 Tembia became the territorial bull at the Majekwe weir part of the Turgwe River.

By then he was an adult and growing to be a big bull of probably about 3 tons, like his father. Over the years I actually watched him mate with over 18 females, and saw the calves born from those events. He was never an aggressive bull, and he would gape for my camera when I called his name. He had learnt from his father, as Bob really used to show off to me.

Tembia and I had known one another since his birth; he knew that I was part of the pod in so many ways. When I had to feed the hippos during droughts he led the females to my feeding stations. When I arrived with visitors to show them the hippos resting on a sandbank, the females and calves would get a fright and immediately prepare to flee back into the safety of the water. I would quickly call out to Tembia and he would realise it was me and simply relax; his attitude calmed the females, assuring them that the visitors were nothing out of the ordinary. So many volunteers got to meet Tembia's family at very close quarters thanks to his gentle nature, something I am sure he inherited from Bob, the first hippo that had openly accepted me.

Then, in December 2022, word reached me that a hippo had been shot. Next, I received a report that two more hippo carcasses had been seen. I couldn't get anything more from the informant as the people involved had clammed up. I had no idea of the victims' sex or size, just that two more were dead. For six months I had been noting erratic behaviour among the hippos at Tembia's pool. It's possible that some of the hippos had been close to where family members were shot, or had even witnessed brutality. Hippos, like many animals, grieve the death of one of their family. I have watched on several occasions and photographed hippos licking and standing by a dead family member, sometimes for up to a week. They eventually move away once the carcass has been set upon by scavengers and is no longer recognisable as a hippo. Now Tembia, their dominant bull, was absent.

Every year for about two months during the rains, Tembia and some of his family would move to another pool upstream. It is adjacent to a property within the Save Valley Conservancy that was stolen from the rightful owners during the land invasions. The woman who claimed the land was high up in the Zimbabwe government hierarchy, and therefore untouchable; and when she later died, her daughter took over the property. Hundreds of wild animals have been slaughtered on that land since it was taken over. Two rhinos, which are protected animals in Zimbabwe, were found not only shot dead and with their horns removed, but buried. Who buries a rhino? – only someone who knows they are operating illegally and who doesn't want evidence against them lying around.

This time, Tembia didn't come back. Several of his females have, since December, been seen, then gone away, and then come back again. I am still not one hundred percent sure of who is gone for good. But I think now that Tembia was killed in December. Seven shots were heard at the time of the report that a young female had been dragged out of the river. No other remains were found in the vicinity, so Tembia and one other hippo must have been wounded and moved away, and died later from their wounds. This knowledge brings on a hollowness and emptiness in my stomach, pain throughout my entire body and tears that can no longer flow – Africa has exhausted my supply.

The reason I suspect that Tembia has died is that Kuchek has now turned up at Tembia's pool, six kilometres from the house, and has taken over Tembia's family. He must have known, in that mysterious way that hippos do, that the territorial bull was no longer there. Kuchek now has a large family to preside over. His 'own' two females are at present still in our area but, with time, I wouldn't be at all surprised if they went to join him. Then, for the first time in over 30 years I will have not one single hippo near our home ... unless young Steve moves here and becomes the youngest bull to have his own territory. Only time will tell.

I had known Tembia for nearly 30 years, and many people in distant countries had adopted him in that time, which is one of the ways we raise funds to help the hippos. One sponsor, in particular, stands out, as he was just a little boy when he adopted Tembia. I met Simeon with his mother in the UK when I went over to give hippo presentations at various universities. Simeon is now an adult, a father and a policeman, and he has just written this to me – it sums up so much:

'Hi Karen,

This is terribly sad news and upset me when I read it last night whilst at work. I can tell from your letter just how upset you are too.

I've been trying to work out how long I have sponsored Tembia. I can't remember but I wondered if you have any records. I think I was around the age of 7–10 which would have been around 1995–1998?

I remember the evening my parents first told me they had sponsored Tembia. As a young boy who loved (and still loves) hippos it was really special. I loved reading and learning all about Tembia and how special he was having been first born after the drought.

Eventually, as I got older and became an 'adult' I took over the payment of Tembia and continued to enjoy seeing the pictures, videos and newsletters. Tembia meant a huge amount to me as well, which is why I continued to sponsor him.

I always dreamt I would one day come to Zimbabwe and see Tembia in the flesh. I feel really sad that can never be a reality because of the selfish, vile acting of poaching! Tembia always struck me as a strong, handsome, confident alpha male, but not even that could protect him from human interference.

I am so terribly sorry for your loss. I know he meant so much to you and you worked so hard just to keep the hippos alive all those years ago so Tembia could be born. Since then your work has time and time again saved Tembia and the other hippos ...'

His words have helped keep me focused and able to continue doing my best for these hippos and all the other local wild animals. People round the world who also love these hippos form a support base, and this is a major part of what keeps me going.

21

Animals in my life

The animals in our lives keep us focused on the present, give us something to live for other than ourselves, and heighten our sense of responsibility – not only for their welfare, but also for our own. Many years ago when I spent a while living in Holland with Jean-Roger, I remember seeing a very old man with an equally old dog pass by our apartment every day. Both had wobbly limbs, bent backs and a very slow shuffle, and yet they had each other – a good reason for both to carry on. I think it criminal when elderly people enter care homes and are not allowed to take their beloved pets with them, at a time when they need them most. There have been times in my life that have been extremely hard to cope with, times when only Squiggle mongoose or Steve hippo have helped me keep my head above water.

Once when a spider bit me and I became extremely ill, I knew I couldn't give up because Squiggle needed me. Jean-Roger, I felt, would always be able to pick himself up and continue his life without me – but Squiggle depended on me for her continued existence. Here in the bush there are always wild animals in need, and this validates us – we work for them and with them. I feel enormous anxiety when a familiar animal goes missing. I worry constantly and spend most of my waking hours trying to figure out what could have happened to it. And still it is worth it to me to care for and love these animals. The rewards are great, both for me and the animals I manage to help.

Recently, a little female warthog, Baba Girl, turned up with an injured foot: part of the hoof on one leg was torn off, possibly on a rock or by a predator. I spent quite a few weeks dabbing aloe vera on the foot; and now the hoof shell has regrown and it looks practically normal. A further reward for us has been her recent arrival with a baby piglet, which is unusual for such a young warthog. It is a triumph that so many warthogs have survived, and we hope most of their piglets will grow to adulthood too, restocking our area. Many warthogs are now regulars at Hippo Haven, along with any number of baboons – perhaps we should change our name to Hog and Baboon Haven!

Now it's our job to keep these animals safe, an ongoing necessity as poaching in our area never stops. But, although at times the incursions and slaughter are soul destroying, and the counter-measures a huge financial drain on the Trust, we do not even consider giving up or giving in.

In the 2000s there was an anthrax outbreak in our area, putting our hippos at risk, with a strong chance that more than half of the population could have died. I arranged for all the hippos to be vaccinated, and we didn't lose any. There are 21 hippos here at present, but 68 calves have been born since I first embarked on this journey and found my vocation. Many of the calves, when older, have dispersed to other river systems, which has helped grow the hippo population further afield within the Conservancy.

Over the years we have faced people pressures, hunting, poaching, land takeovers, natural disasters such as the anthrax outbreak and, lately, some high-up officials shooting three hippos illegally – and so it goes on.

However, I have to keep looking forward. I tell myself that without my original intervention during the 1992 drought, not one hippo would have survived within the Turgwe River; and that since saving those 13 hippos, their numbers (and distribution) have grown. I know that my beloved Squiggle had a good, long life, and that just over nine years is about the time mongooses are ready to move on.

As with anything worthwhile in life, there will be hardships and days of pain and frustration, but you square your shoulders and you look on the positive side: to healthy, happy hippos and all the other wildlife under our watch. Here at Hippo Haven, our wild friends are not just animals, they are company for us – part of our social circle – and they make us laugh daily.

My late mum always said to me, 'Karen, you cannot help every animal or every living thing. What you have to do is concentrate on your own garden and what lives in that.'

I define my garden as anywhere the hippos live and graze; that is the area I protect. Thanks now to the loyalty of my husband, who is mostly by my side, and driven by my commitment to these amazing animals, the Turgwe Hippo Trust has flourished.